Strategic Planning for Library Multitype Cooperatives: Samples & Examples

ASCLA Changing Horizons Series # 1

edited by

Steven A. Baughman

Elizabeth A. Curry

Association of Specialized and Cooperative Library Agencies
American Library Association
Chicago
1997

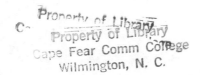

Cover: Align Design

Printed on 50-pound Arbor Smooth paper, pH-neutral stocks;
bound in 10-point C1S cover stock by Batson Printing Inc.

The paper used in this publication meets the minimum
requirements of American National Standard for
Information Sciences--Permanence of Paper for
Printed Library Materials, ANSI Z39.48-1992.

ISBN 0-8389-7914-9

Printed in the United States of America

99 98 97   3 2 1

TABLE OF CONTENTS

**Strategic Planning for Library Multitype Cooperatives:
Samples & Examples**

ASCLA Changing Horizons Series # 1

ACKNOWLEDGMENTS

This publication was a collaborative effort, the result of the enthusiasm, energy, insights and dedication of many people. We especially want to thank the library cooperatives, systems, networks and state library agencies which sent their plans to us. The participation of these organizations was essential to the success of this project. This is another example of the power of resource sharing.

The organizational requirements for this document involved many people. It was a real team effort. We appreciate everyone's contribution.

Margaret C. Miller, the production coordinator, deserves special recognition for her many days of work to prepare and format the document. Her dedication, her patience and her attention to detail were our foundation. She made it possible to present samples from over fifty different plans with fifty different formats. She made this book a cohesive document which we think will make a difference in shaping future library services.

Roxanna Blackwell from SOLINET handled the mailings, maintained the database of contacts, gathered the plans and compiled the list of references.

Catherine Wilt from AMIGOS readily volunteered to be the proofreader.

Elizabeth Zarelli and Paula Manrique from SEFLIN assisted in many ways with the preparation of the manuscript and distribution of the review copies.

Lillian Lewis, our ASCLA staff liaison coordinated the cover art and printing.

ASCLA Publication Committee and the ICAN Executive Committee members contributed their ideas, encouragement and support.

We also want to acknowledge the collaborative working relationship we had as editors. We took turns encouraging each other and empowering each other. We kept our perspective and avoided the temptation to focus on minutia. Our sense of humor and our respect for each other made it possible for us to complete this publication.

Steven A. Baughman

Elizabeth A. Curry

INTRODUCTION

As interlibrary cooperation has proliferated in the last several decades, multitype library organizations and systems have emerged as important forces in librarianship. Ranging from multi-state regional networks to local area consortia, the need for thoughtful and organized strategic planning has been recognized as an important cornerstone for organizational success. Libraries and cooperatives have a long tradition of developing long range and operational plans but the strategic perspective has been increasingly recognized as critical. The environment in which libraries and cooperatives operate continues to change rapidly. The level of preparedness for undertaking this complex process has been widely variable. The results, not unexpectedly, have been equally variable. Where there have been sufficient resources, outside planning consultants have been utilized, but even in these cases the results have not always met expectations. A key concept is that different organizations are at different stages in development and we all need to continue to work on honing process and product. Our effort in this publication is to show the wide range of development reflected in the planning documents of cooperatives and systems of varying sizes.

Planning for library cooperatives and systems is a process which is indeed unique. It necessarily draws upon the planning literature of the corporate world, academia and librarianship. The process is characterized by a delicate yet essential balance with many levels of involvement. The input of diverse individuals with a variety of relationships is critical. The library cooperative's staff, member library management and staff, as well as, end user constituencies all have interest in organizational direction and services. Typically, many of the individuals who come to the table of multitype planning are either planning novices or have experience only within a very focused component. The quest for more expertise in strategic thinking and planning is not limited to libraries and cooperatives. Leaders in business, education, government and community organizations are striving to develop the strategic advantage. Many times it is a question of survival for a business or an organization. Broadening the vision, building skills and achieving consensus are necessary parts which emerge but which are not normally, strictly speaking, planning. Navigating the complexities of the process requires extraordinary talent which draws upon skills in the political, communications, research, business, economic, marketing, technical and service provision arenas. The shoals are many, but the rewards are great.

Recognizing the need for a guide to help those associated with library cooperative organizations, the Interlibrary Cooperation and Networking Section of the Association for Cooperative and Specialized Library Agencies within the American Library Association directed two publications and a pre-conference be developed to address this requirement. The purpose of this project is to provide some of the needed definition, knowledge and experience base to library cooperatives embarking on a strategic planning process.

Two volumes are planned -- companion pieces -- which are also the beginning of the new ASCLA Changing Horizons series. This book, *Strategic Planning for Library Multitype Cooperatives: Samples & Examples,* presents an overview of the current status of library multitype cooperatives in the United States: the missions, visions, values, environmental trends, goals, objectives and strategies. *Samples & Examples* could be used as an introduction to library cooperatives, as a discussion guide or as a comparative tool. This book is designed to be used as a collection of "possibilities" for organizations to review as part of their planning. The companion volume, *Strategic Planning for Library Multitype Cooperatives: A Planning Process*, to be published Spring 1998, will be a handbook to be used by organizations as they structure their strategic planning process. These publications are designed to be the foundation for the pre-conference.

This volume, *Strategic Planning for Library Multitype Cooperatives: Samples & Examples,* draws heavily upon the existing experience base as it presents a range of sample planning document components drawn from the 58 plans submitted in response to a nationwide mail request. This original mailing went to a list of 243 library cooperatives, networks and systems in the United States culled from several national directory tools. The planning documents cited were current as of December 1996, when they were submitted. It should be noted, however, the time span covered by specific documents varies rather widely, depending upon where a particular organization was at the time of our request for submission of their document.

Selection from the submitted plans was conducted by the two editors independently. A meeting was then held to review the results of this work. A surprising congruence of choices for the various component parts was the result. In almost all areas, the documents chosen as representative examples were on both editors' lists. A process of reviewing and culling followed in order to present *representative* samples from the wide range of possibilities. In many cases, similarities were noted and one representative was chosen as the example of this approach. It should be emphasized that a particular document's omission from this collection does not indicate that the examples used better represent a given approach. Decisions relating to presentation of the samples were made in order to insure that some of the flavor of the original formatting was retained without the clutter of multiple margins, fonts and graphical components. Chapter 9 is the section where the formatting and design of the information is highlighted.

The accompanying reference list of the plans submitted includes address information for additional contact with the organizations which participated in this publication. A growing trend among library cooperatives is mounting planning documents on the World Wide Web. A limited number of URLs which were submitted to this publication included strategic plans. These are listed in Chapter 9. It seems likely that more and more organizations will include strategic plans in their Web pages. Readers are encouraged to check the Web sites of organizations of interest since organizations may have posted current planning documents subsequent to this publication.

CHAPTER 1

CONTENTS PAGES

Each cooperative, system or network designs a planning process which best fits the needs of the organization. In the same way, the structure of the planning document reflects the needs of the organization. The purpose of the planning process and the environmental circumstances of the group will impact the format of the document. The differences in the organization of the documents show varied approaches. The funding source of the planning process affects the final outline of the document. The primary and secondary target audiences for the plan also dictate format. For instance, State Library Agencies have plans to meet the requirements for administration of federal grants. Sections of the plans address interlibrary cooperation and networking. Some State Library Agencies also have state-wide multitype networking plans or technology plans. The table of contents is the outline and structure of the document. A comprehensive and well organized table of contents allows people to:

- quickly evaluate the scope of the document and planning process,
- easily locate the sections of information they need,
- use the document for frequent reference.

The samples in this chapter show tables of contents which contain the basic Purpose, Mission, Vision, Environment, Goals and Objectives. There are differences in what is placed in the appendices. Groups varied widely on the length of the description of their organization, the history or governance. In some cases, it would seem the group assumed everyone reading the document knew this background. Generally, the member libraries, board and participants in the planning process were acknowledged. The planning process was described in many plans, but the depth of information varied. Some groups reviewed their accomplishments since the last plan or commented on the present programs of service. Some groups reported on the SWOT process (strengths, weaknesses, opportunities, threats). Only a few plans included a high level of detail on the resources required, budgeting or financial planning. The specific finances or exact type of technology is perhaps more appropriate to an annual plan of service than a strategic plan. However, it is likely a cooperative, system or network may need that information for their strategic plan to move forward at a certain point in the organization's development. The trends in the external environment and the broad impact of technological changes are increasingly being addressed in a major portion of the strategic plan. Public policy issues and questions are critical. Relationships and partnerships, particularly outside the library or cooperative, are also becoming important to strategic planning.

It should be noted that some groups publish two documents as part of the planning process: (1) the background environmental analysis, SWOT and information from focus groups or planning task forces and (2) the strategic planning directions which resulted from the background discussions. The samples in this publication are generally from the second type of planning document; but, the reader should remember there could be other materials which the organizations compiled separately.

TABLE OF CONTENTS

#10 b. -- Central Jersey Regional Library Cooperative

TABLE OF CONTENTS

55 b. -- Tampa Bay Library Consortium, Inc.

Table of Contents

#30 -- Minuteman Library Network

Table of Contents

Attachments
Board of Directors
Planning Committee Members
Action Plans

#9 -- Central Florida Library Cooperative

Table of Contents

#43 -- PALINET

Table of Contents

#17 -- Florida Network Planning Task Force and the State Library of Florida

Table of Contents

#21 -- Indiana State Library

TABLE OF CONTENTS

#27 -- Michigan Library Association

Contents

#6 -- California State Library

8

CHAPTER 2

PLANNING PROCESS

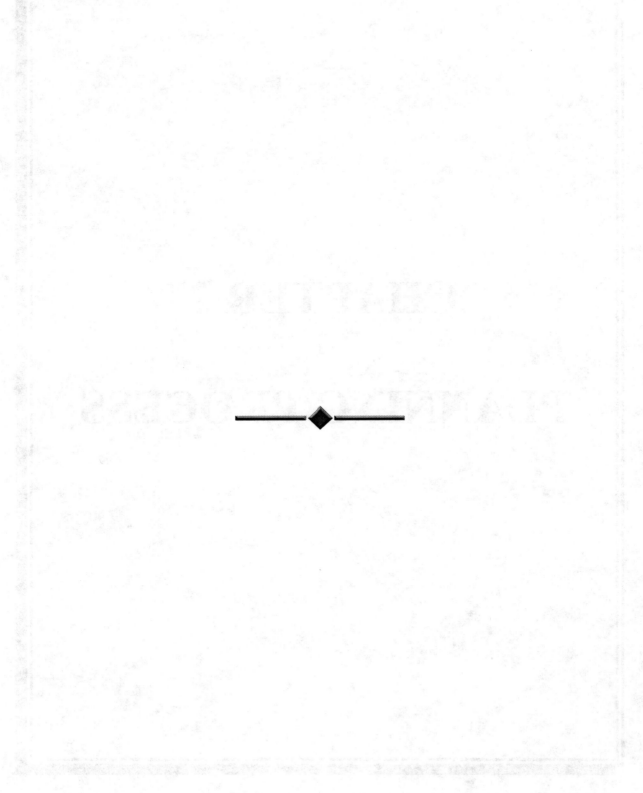

PLANNING PROCESS

Strategic planning is a complex process requiring much preparation and organization. It is more of an art than a science. In the library cooperative environment, it is almost always surrounded by power, politics and individual agendas. Having a process established for organizational planning is fundamental both for establishing realistic expectations among all participants, as well as, insuring that the results of the process are of maximum utility. Key pieces of an organization's planning process can be elements such as: the planning schedule and cycle, the roles and responsibilities for planning, accountability and on-going review and evaluation techniques.

Having the library cooperative or system's planning process documented can provide a number of benefits:
- The approach can be easily replicated and updated for the next cycle, not reinvented.
- While the planning team participants may be all new, continuity with past planning efforts can insure a consistent result.
- As the review process goes forward from the planning document, weaknesses in the process may be revealed which can drive changes in the documentation.

Some of the planning documents make reference to the process used to produce them. In a number of cases, either by reference or inference, it is clear the articulation of the organization's planning process is to be found in separate documents. What actually appears in the plan itself is often a summary of that process with acknowledgments to the particular planning team which produced it.

A common element noted in the submitted plans was the brief overview of the approach and calendar associated with the plan's production. The make up of the planning team was another common element. Historical or external documents (for example, statewide plans) that were critical to the plan's development are often cited in order to provide context for interpretation of the plan itself. Methodology elements, such as (1) the use of a survey instrument or process and (2) the employment of an outside consultant to facilitate the process, are also commonly present. Provisions for plan maintenance and updating are incorporated in some form as well. In one plan, the interesting approach of incorporating the planning process as a goal for the cooperative was noted.

Planning

The Massachusetts Board of Library Commissioners is the agency of state government with the statutory authority and responsibility to organize, develop, coordinate, regulate and improve library services throughout the Commonwealth. The agency operates under a Board which consists of nine Commissioners appointed by the Governor.

In October 1992, the Board approved the formation of a Strategic Planning Committee. This thirty-one-member committee, which contained representation from libraries of all types, all sizes, and from all geographic areas of the Commonwealth, was charged to:

1. Analyze the current environment for library services and current strengths and weaknesses in library services for the people of the Commonwealth;
2. Create a collective vision of future library services for the people of the Commonwealth in the year 2000 and beyond;
3. Develop a strategic plan for the future of library service provided to the people of the Commonwealth by libraries of all types.

This plan, which was developed by the Committee with broad participation from the library community, represents the Board's vision of the library services that must be available to all residents of the Commonwealth if they are to meet the challenges of the future.

The plan is strategic, in that it focuses on what must be accomplished, rather than detailing at length all of the specifics of how it will be achieved. Specific implementation plans, addressing statutory, regulatory, programmatic, technological, and funding issues need to be developed, implemented, evaluated and refined on an ongoing basis in order to accomplish the goals and objectives contained in the plan.

In large part, the development of the plan is the direct result of the work of the citizens, elected officials, library trustees and librarians who participated in the 1991 White House Conference on Library and Information Services. This group set as a top priority that the Board of Library Commissioners create a strategic plan to guide the development of future library services in a time of rapid changes in technology and user needs.

July 1993

#26 -- Massachusetts Board of Library Commissioners

PREFACE

In March of 1994, the Central Jersey Regional Library Cooperative organized a task force to develop a strategic plan for the Cooperative in the area of automation and technology. The task force began its work in May and completed it in October.

This planning process was a direct outcome of the **Region V Library Cooperative Long Range Strategic Plan, 1993-1998**. In addition, documents such as the **Report on the Reference Planning Project**, completed by Nancy Bolt of JNR Associates, and "Access to Information Resources -- Information Strategies for the Regional Library Cooperatives of New Jersey," prepared by RMG Consultants for the Directors of the RLCs, served as background material that informed some of the ideas in the plan.

In order to ensure an effective planning process, the Cooperative contracted with DocuMentors, an independent consulting firm in Rockaway, New Jersey, to facilitate our planning. Dr. John M. Cohn and Ms. Ann L. Kelsey worked with the task force chairperson and myself in planning, organizing and facilitating the meetings of the task force.

The Cooperative extends a special thanks to all the task force members, whose names and affiliations are listed on the following page, for the time and effort they contributed to the process and its outcome. It was a successful undertaking, one which we hope will serve to guide the Cooperative, benefit its members and contribute to strengthening the New Jersey Library Network.

#10 b. -- Central Jersey Regional Library Cooperative

13

An Overview of the Planning Process

The Central Florida Library Consortium has a historical commitment to being a member driven organization. In keeping with this ideal, the membership was very involved with developing this most recent strategic plan for the organization's future.

In December 1994 the first meeting of the Planning Committee was held. The committee was composed of representatives from each library type; State University, Community College, Private Academic, County Public, Municipal Public and Special Library. The Committee felt it was necessary to hear directly from the membership their vision of the future of the Consortium. A "town meeting" was planned to meet this objective. The meeting was held at the Seminole Public Library. It was attended by individual librarians from a broad cross section of member institutions. Ideas were shared and some basic goals for the Consortium were recorded. These goals were ranked by attendees before the meeting concluded. Objectives were also established under each of these goals.

Committee and Interest Group Chairs were asked to poll their members and to provide information to the Planning Committee about issues of concern. Additionally, two surveys were sent to member delegates asking delegates to rank goals and specific projects. One survey was sent before the "Town Meeting" with a list (including definitions) of the goals identified in the <u>Florida Plan for Interlibrary Cooperation, Resource Sharing and Network Development</u>. Ranking of the goals was then tabulated. When the results of the "Town Meeting" were organized and tabulated, the membership was re-polled to solicit information on establishing priorities for the specific objectives developed at the meeting. The results of these surveys were included in the Committee's deliberations.

All of the aforementioned input was considered by the Committee in the development of the following plan. It is hoped that this plan will provide a framework for CFLC's continued development over the next 5 year period.

#9 -- Central Florida Library Cooperative

INTRODUCTION

At the June 19, 1992 Board of Trustees meeting, the Board authorized a Strategic Planning Task Force to undertake the development of a strategic plan for the South Central Research Library Council. The plan was to extend and build upon the 1991 report of the Executive Director <u>To Connect, to Challenge, to Champion.</u>

Broadly representative of the Board, staff and member libraries, task force members were appointed by the President of the Board.

The task force met on a monthly basis from September, 1992 through June, 1993. We periodically reported to the Board of Trustees and to the membership at large, and sought input from a wide variety of sources. Often we felt as though we were drowning in a sea of unrelated data, observations and opinions. Our final set of seven strategic directions emerged through sheer determination, intellectual discipline and effective participation by all task force members.

We believe that the future is unpredictable, ever-changing and difficult to imagine. We suggest that these seven strategic directions will be useful for a maximum of three years. We recommend that a permanent planning group be established to monitor, review, and revise this plan on an annual basis.

We also encourage all parts of the South Central Research Library Council to continually scan the environment for clues about the future which will affect the South Central Research Library Council and the libraries we serve. Through on-going strategic scanning and planning, the future of this consortium will remain healthy and capable of serving the needs of our members.

#48 -- South Central Research Library Council

THE PLANNING PROCESS

The planning team had the primary responsibility for the development of the objectives recommended to the CCLS Board. The team met four times over a period of five months: December, 1995; and February, March, and May, 1996.

The process included a careful examination and review of:

- the results of the annual survey of CCLS members (September, 1996) (Appendix B);

- The Future of Systems, a paper addressing the future of Colorado Systems, written at the request of the CCLS Board by Gordon Barhydt (Appendix C);

- the Director's annual report to the Board for FY 1995;

- the annual narrative report for the system for FY 1995;

- Strategies 2001, the Strategic Plan for Library Services in Colorado; and

- the FY 1996 CCLS budget

The planning team developed a three year vision of CCLS, a list of key stakeholders, identified organizational strengths and weaknesses and examined opportunities and barriers from outside the organization.

The planning team also developed a model of system services (Appendix D), identifying primary and secondary clients for system services, strategic directions for CCLS and the interrelationship of strategic directions and objectives.

The primary clients for the Central Colorado Library System are the member and associate member libraries (academic, public, school and special).

The planning team selected a set of preliminary objectives for analysis and CCLS staff conducted a gap analysis of the proposed objectives (an assessment of staff time, dollars and other resources necessary to achieve the objectives). On the basis of the gap analysis the planning team made recommendations to the CCLS Board for specific objectives for 1997. Objectives are also proposed for fiscal years 1998 and 1999 although it should be recognized that projections beyond FY 1997 are influenced by the dynamic changes in the system and its member libraries.

#8 -- Central Colorado Library System

BACKGROUND

The New Hampshire Automated Information System (NHAIS) marks its tenth anniversary this year. In 1982 the New Hampshire Automation Task Force made a recommendation to "consider an online, statewide union catalog when it is realistic and affordable."(1) Two years later in January of 1984 the first computer used for the union list was installed at the State Library. The system grew rapidly after that, fueled by an expanding economy, growing interest in library automation by libraries, and major developments in computer and telecommunications technology.

By the end of the 1980's, it had become evident that even more dramatic changes in library technology, the economy, and the information marketplace required an analysis of past activities and a plan for the future direction of NHAIS.

On December 20, 1990, the Automation Planning & Review Committee presented their final report (2) to the New Hampshire Automated Information Systems Board. The committee had been established in 1989 by Shirley Adamovich, Commissioner of Cultural Affairs, to examine the NHAIS system and to make recommendations which would set directions for the next several years.

The Automation Planning & Review Committee convened in June 1989 and decided to take a broad look at the NHAIS system. The committee looked at how NHAIS was operating, where it was headed, and what courses of action might be necessary to strengthen and expand the network. Using the Kotler/Murphy strategic planning model, the committee systematically examined internal and external environments that affected NHAIS, analyzed what threats and opportunities were facing the system, conducted a review of the system's resources, examined the mission and goal structure, and made recommendations.

In 1991 a subcommittee of the NHAIS Board was established to review the Automation Planning & Review Committee's report and extract those elements which should be addressed in a long range plan. That report was presented to the NHAIS Board in September of the same year.

This strategic plan is based on the report of the subcommittee, the Automation Planning & Review Committee Report, the recommendations of the New Hampshire Conference on Libraries and Information Services (3), and the Long-Range Program for Library Service (4). Many of the governance issues identified by the Automation Planning & Review Committee were addressed in the 1992 session of the Legislature and thus are not included in this plan.

....

(1) *New Hampshire Automation Task Force Final Report* by Carol Nelson, Project Administrator (New Hampshire State Library, 1982) p.1.
(2) *Report of the Automation Planning & Review Committee* by John Courtney, Chair (New Hampshire State Library, October 1990).
(3) *New Hampshire State Conference on Libraries and Information Services*, February 14 & 15, 1992, Final Report. (New Hampshire State Library, June 1991).
(4) *Long-Range Program for Library Service*, 1991-1995. (New Hampshire State Library, October 1990).

#35 -- New Hampshire State Library

GOAL 1: Planning

TBLC and the area library community will cooperatively plan to provide library resource sharing and network development among TBLC libraries.

Objective 1. The Planning Committee will gather input from Member libraries and the Board of Directors on library resource sharing needs and statewide planning.

Objective 2 The Planning Committee will take a leadership role in implementing and publicizing the goals of the TBLC Strategic Plan.

Objective 3. The Finance Committee and Executive Director will evaluate and recommend revisions to the financial plan.

Objective 4. A Marketing Committee will be formed to develop and implement a TBLC Marketing Plan which will demonstrate to funding agencies and the public the value of resource sharing.

Objective 5. The Legislative Advocacy Committee will serve as a legislative liaison at the local, state and national levels.

PLANNING ONGOING ACTION PLANS 1995/96 through 1999/00

TIMELINE	ACTION PLAN	RESPONSIBILITY
Ongoing	Maintain a reserve fund of at least $150,000 to strengthen the financial stability of TBLC	Executive Director
November-December	Evaluate and revise the TBLC Financial Plan	Financial Committee
By March	Evaluate and revise TBLC's Strategic Plan	Planning Committee
March - April	Review and revise all service fee schedules	Financial Committee
March - April	Review annual reserve fund targets	Financial Committee
March - April	Recommend to the Board of Directors dues for fiscal year after next. (e.g. in Mar. '96 recommend 97-98 dues)	Financial Committee
April - May	Review appropriate staffing levels and space to support Membership	Executive Director
By October	Develop TBLC financial plan	Financial Committee and Executive Director
By October	Establish annual reserve fund targets for TBLC	Financial Committee
November	Vote on dues at annual membership meeting	President/TBLC
November	Solicit input for Strategic Plan to membership at annual meeting	Planning Committee
Throughout the year	Develop competitive grant proposals - project goals to be developed	Executive Director
Throughout the year	Budget for and participate in membership in civic and leadership organizations	Executive Director
Throughout the year	Advocate for libraries at the local, state and national levels	Legislative Committee

18

PLANNING ACTION PLANS 1995/96 and 1996/97

TIMELINE	ACTION PLAN	RESPONSIBILITY
October 1995 (Done in Dec. 1995	Hold membership brainstorming session ("What should TBLC look like in the Year 2000?"; Elizabeth Curry, Facilitator)	Planning Committee
January 1996	Appoint a Marketing Committee	President
February - March 1996	Set Annual Membership targets (review potential) for full and enhanced members by type of library	Membership Committee
February - March 1996	Discuss dues and fees structure and report to Financial Committee	Membership Committee
March 1996	Recommend dues and fees levels to the Board of Directors for the 1997-98 year	Financial Committee
By July 1996	Develop a marketing plan	Marketing Committee
August 1996	Present marketing plan to the Board	Marketing Committee
By September 1996	Establish a speaker's bureau	Marketing Committee
By October 1996	Gather data on financial planning for non-profit organizations	Financial Committee
January 1997 Onward	Market to TBLC library constituency and general public as outlined in the plan	Marketing Committee
February 1997	Budget for implementation of marketing plan	Executive Director
March 1997	Recommend dues and fees levels to the Board of Directors for the 1998-99 year	Financial Committee
June 1997	Budget for Strategic Planning process for 1998/99	Executive Director
By September 1997	Produce marketing and public relations material for use with general public	Marketing Committee

#55 a. -- *Tampa Bay Library Consortium, Inc.*

CHAPTER 3

VALUES
&
PHILOSOPHY

VALUES & PHILOSOPHY

The ways in which an organization is able to articulate the essential foundations of its organizational culture are critical to successful communication within the planning process and beyond. Every organization has a culture and bedrock of fundamental beliefs. These may reflect the values of the founding organizations or may represent the sometimes competing values held by a number of influential stakeholders who guide the organization. Over time, the dynamics of the organization and its position in the environment change. For library cooperatives, these kinds of changes are increasingly common and should drive a frequent re-evaluation of the organizational culture, values and principles. In addition, some observers of organizations believe all organizations go through specific developmental stages that require changes and adaptations in the organizational culture if the organization is to remain effective.

Clearly, if a library cooperative is to be effective in the long range, the cultural values of the organization, its staff, management and its members must all be in general agreement. The process of planning itself may uncover differences in values. For example, cooperatives may stress service quality over breadth or over expediency in the delivery of library services.

In the review of submitted planning documents, it was interesting to note that many organizations opted not to include this section -- either as part of the process, or as a component of the final document. While Mission Statements were ubiquitous, articulations of values or guiding principles were not. The examples included in this section offer an interesting range of approaches to the articulation of values. From fairly dense text explanations to bulleted headings with detail, the organizations settled on anywhere from four to eleven statements. Included here are elements called principles, philosophy and values. An interesting definitional problem emerged in a number of the documents examined: a blurring of distinction between the values and the functions of the organization. What the organization *does* became what it valued.

Common areas noted in the value statements included placing value on information in terms of its fundamental value to society, unlimited access and freedom of expression, as well as, open transmission of information. Another commonly held value was equity within the cooperative, which is not dependent upon an equal sharing of the financial burden. Large libraries see a responsibility to the smaller ones and the results of the cooperative's services are not always quantifiable or equitable. Often, a high value was placed upon the cooperative's leadership function, including its proactive search for partnerships. Knowledgeable staff and quality service go hand-in-hand and were often cited as primary values to be nurtured. Also the membership concept, including the basic foundation of member loyalty and support, was often cited.

23

Values

The Worcester Area Cooperating Libraries believes that:

- Users of WACL libraries deserve quality services and collections.
- Diversity in member institutions' size and character contributes to the strength of the organization.
- The collections of the consortium libraries enable each member library to support self-development, education, and scholarly research for its users.
- The consortium has an essential role to play in providing to its constituency effective access to and utilization of information.
- Cooperative efforts are intrinsic to the successful delivery of information to Consortium libraries' users.
- The sense of equity within the consortium does not depend on an exact balance of trade.
- Cooperative research and development in application of information technology enhances service and realizes cost efficiencies.
- Staff development and interaction enhance the quality of service provided to the users.
- Collaboration and sharing strengthen our ability to obtain and provide resources.
- The success of the Worcester Area Cooperating Libraries is advanced by the understanding and commitment of the member institutions' administrators.
- Consortium membership enhances the value of each library to its own users.

#58 -- Worcester Area Cooperating Libraries

VALUES

A. **Quality**
   The South Carolina State Library endeavors to provide services of the highest quality.

B. **Knowledge**
   The South Carolina State Library believes that a well-trained and knowledgeable staff is its greatest asset.

C. **Freedom Of Information**
   The South Carolina State Library believes freedom of expression is a fundamental right of a democratic society and supports the Library Bill of Rights and the Freedom to Read Statement.

D. **Access To Information**
   The South Carolina State Library believes that all citizens regardless of their location or means should have access to library and information services.

E. **Equitable Treatment**
   The South Carolina State Library provides services to its customers in a fair and unbiased manner.

#47 -- South Carolina State Library

SEFLIN VALUES

Leadership
We believe that SEFLIN's leadership is a shared responsibility of all members. We are a member-driven organization that relies on the participation and initiative of every single member of our organization to accomplish shared goals.

Communication
We maintain constant communication with the Southeast Florida library community and respond to member needs in a timely manner.

Innovation
We are committed to providing the best possible service to library customers through the development of innovative methods that result in new and effective library service.

Resource Sharing
We believe that resource sharing is an important and vital component of SEFLIN's program. We are committed to maintaining the strength of local library resources while developing new ways to expand the availability of those resources to residents of Southeast Florida.

Staff
We are committed to providing our members with quality staff who have a broad range of experience to support SEFLIN programs and member needs. Our staff work as a team, respect each other's work and fully participate in the decision making process.

Membership
We recognize that SEFLIN's strength is dependent on the diverse nature of its members. We provide a strong committee structure that encourages our members to participate in network planning and program implementation.

Organization
Our members and staff support and are committed to SEFLIN's mission and program initiatives. We work hard to maintain a sense of humor and perspective about our organization and seek consensus in making decisions. We maintain a quality organization through policies, programs and staff that will benefit the entire Southeast Florida community.

#50 b. -- Southeast Florida Library Information Network, Inc.
(Summary)

HIGH PLAINS REGIONAL LIBRARY SERVICE SYSTEM
PHILOSOPHY OF SERVICE

1. High Plains members are both independent and interdependent.

2. Few if any High Plains programs benefit every member, but each member does benefit in different ways from membership.

3. High Plains helps members make intelligent and appropriate use of existing and emerging technology through whatever action is suitable to the situation, while taking into account the member's need, level of expertise, learning style, and best way to convey the information.

4. Internet Service Providers abound in the High Plains area, and reasonable prices can be negotiated for access. High Plains will help members find, use, install, implement, and integrate Internet service in their libraries and media centers, but there is no need at this time for High Plains to provide that access.

5. The use of technology as a tool is necessary for High Plains and every member library. It is a way to convey information, a way to access information. While it may be frustrating, wonderful, demanding, and efficient, it is of no greater importance than many other facets of service. The immediate need for knowledge and keeping abreast of trends, issues, and development may be greater, but technology shouldn't eclipse the need for maintaining strong foundation services and practices.

6. Every community and school, every child and adult has a right to library services and information. While local resources may be limited (by funding, geographic location, size, role selection, and/or design), the scope of what's available through co-operation should be limitless. Each library will be encouraged to provide the best service possible, and will be respected for what they can do... not denigrated for what they can't do.

7. High Plains provides some services for members which cannot be measured, and quantifiable results cannot be determined. Calming a distraught member after an ugly confrontation with a city manager, counseling someone in strategy for dealing with a problem employee, validating an independently devised process or policy are all examples of extremely important, if unheralded responsibilities. High Plains staff will always cooperate in the collection of data and statistics, but it is understood that a significant portion of our work is not reflected in reports.

8. The strength of the System lies in its ability to react quickly and unbureaucratically to local and regional needs and opportunities. High Plains staff and board have unfailing commitment to assisting members in whatever manner is appropriate, and all service decisions are based on that dedication.

9. The High Plains Long Range Plan and Annual Program/Budget are guidelines for the board, staff, and members. This agency welcomes, in fact seeks out, appropriate opportunities to expand and direct services to members, including cooperative ventures. Lack of inclusion in this document does not in any way signify non-support for a program, activity, or campaign.

#20 -- High Plains Regional Library Service System

CORE VALUES/GUIDING PRINCIPLES

DEFINITION: "Core Values/Guiding Principles are fundamental ethical, moral and professional business beliefs that guide organizational decisions. They describe the organization's desired culture, management style and methods of operation. They are clear and meaningful to ALL employees and should be visible and demonstrated." They should be reflected in the manner in which all agency employees conduct daily business, both internal and external.

* * * * *

LEADERSHIP: We are committed to providing strong, visionary leadership that encourages risk-taking; advocates for programs, staff and those we serve; and fosters open supportive communication.

INNOVATION: We are committed to proactive, creative and strategic approaches in the continuous evaluation and improvement of our services.

QUALITY SERVICE: We are committed to providing customers with equitable access to timely and reliable services.

PROFESSIONALISM: We are an expert and principled work force which treats customers and colleagues with respect, honesty and integrity in a spirit of cooperation.

#23 -- Kentucky Department for Libraries & Archives

Guiding Principles

*P*rovide cost-effective technology-based services responsive to the needs of libraries and other consumers of information, and exercise regular review and update of service lines to ensure that locally developed or brokered products continue to meet the needs of members.

*P*romote, develop, and support programs devoted to preservation and cooperative use of member resources.

*P*rovide cost-effective, innovative training and support programs to strengthen libraries' implementation of information technologies.

*M*aintain member loyalty and support by meeting member needs in a cooperative, open, and participative manner.

*M*aintain a balanced operating budget with adequate working capital, human resources, and facilities.

#1 -- AMIGOS

VALUES (developed May 1993):

The Boston Library Consortium believes that:

- The collections of the Consortium libraries enable each member library to support scholarly research for its users.

- Consortium membership enhances the value of each library to its own users.

- Cooperative efforts are intrinsic to the successful delivery of information to Consortium libraries' users.

- Diversity in member institutions' size and character contributes to the strength of this democratic organization.

- Cooperative research and development in application of information technology enhances service and realizes cost efficiencies.

- Staff development and interaction enhance the quality of service.

- The tangible assets jointly owned by the Boston Library Consortium should be devoted primarily to the benefit of its constituency.

- The success of the Boston Library Consortium is advanced by the understanding and commitment of the member institutions' administrators.

- The Boston Library Consortium believes that the Consortium has an essential role to play in providing to its constituency, including all citizens of the Commonwealth, effective access to and utilization of information.

ADDITIONAL VALUE (developed May 1996):

- The sense of equity within the Consortium does not depend on an exact balance of trade.

#5 -- Boston Library Consortium

Guiding Principles for Network Planning

The Interim Group developed a set of over-arching principles to guide the network planning process. These principles are:

1. The library user is the primary focus of everything the Network does.
   - Quality of services improves when their design focuses on the needs of those directly receiving services.
   - The needs of the end user are growing beyond the resources of the local library.

2. All network providers will take a cooperative, coordinated approach to networking.
   - The Network organization has the ability and desire to cooperate.
   - The Network will greatly increase fiscal responsibility through cooperation/coordination.
   - The Network will increase the quality and availability of services through cooperation/coordination.

3. The Network will maximize the use of state funds through cooperation and coordination, and it will evaluate ways to maximize the use of other funds.
   - There is an increasing demand from all sectors for fiscal accountability.
   - State funding will remain flat over the foreseeable future.
   - Libraries and the network agencies will compete with commercial and other not-for-profit agencies for delivery of services to the end user.

4. Priority for using state funds will be given to meeting statewide service goals.
   - By profiling its total membership, the Network can design services that are tailored to the specific needs of end users.
   - The Network will offer its services in the context of competitive services and marketplace trends.
   - The Network will survey emerging state and national trends relating to library and information technologies, and track economic, educational, social and demographic trends to assure its priorities are consonant with user needs.

5. The Network structure for service delivery will be responsible to changing needs.
   - Technology is causing service demands to change more rapidly than before.
   - End users and libraries are becoming more demanding and sophisticated with respect to their information needs.
   - The demand for improved service is coming in areas never before considered by libraries, such as users' demand for remote, dial access to on-line systems.
   - Services will be delivered in a manner to cost-effectively reach target audiences.

Guiding Principles for Network Services

1. Network services are delivered to end users through libraries and their parent institutions.

2. Network services are designed to improve connectivity between end users and library and information resources.

3. Network services emphasize stewardship of shared collections in order to provide a virtual, seamless collection to end users within the state.

4. Network services are strengthened through partnerships with libraries and civic, business, government, and other organizations.

5. Network services include an appropriate mix of centralized and decentralized programs that meet the needs of Indiana residents.

#21 -- Indiana State Library

OUR PHILOSOPHY

A flourishing society requires information, cultural memory, and interpretation. The California State Library is uniquely positioned to serve each of these needs and strives to be ever-available as a resource to Californians as they seek to understand the past, cope with the present, and forge the future.

In order to meet the information needs of government, other libraries, and the people, our services to Californians must be proactive as well as reactive. Not only must we meet the immediately expressed needs of our customers, we must also anticipate where state government is going, ask the appropriate questions, formulate the correct policies, collect the correct materials, so that we might offer instant and applicable information service to state government and the public as required.

This implies that the individual staff members of the California State Library will themselves be intellectually engaged with the world around them; that they will have a sense of society, especially a sense of California; that they will reflect upon experience; that they will be readers and analyzers; that they find enjoyment in their jobs and see the intrinsic value of their work, especially how their particular job fits into the pattern of the whole; and that they will bring the fruits of their own intellectual engagement to bear on their professional responsibilities.

The manner in which we work towards our vision is as important as the vision itself. Our central values are key to achieving our vision for the future, and as such, we strive to integrate them into our daily service to state government, the state's libraries, the public, and to each other.

OUR VALUES

Information: We believe that library and information service is essential to a learning society because information and knowledge are indispensable to the development of human potential, the advancement of civilization, and the continuance of enlightened self-government.

Services: We believe our services are a reflection of our people. We will strive for continual improvement in all our activities and to deliver services that are of the highest quality which consistently satisfy our customers' needs.

Partnerships: We believe partnerships that are built on honesty and respect are critical for our success and strive actively to collaborate with all our partners in order to achieve mutual benefit for both ourselves and our partners.

People: We believe that the State Library is only as good as the people we employ and strive to treat our staff members with dignity and respect, encouraging participation, involvement and teamwork at all times and at all levels.

OUR PRIORITIES

Customers: We exist to serve our customers and meeting their needs is first and foremost.

Quality: We value the importance of providing rapid and comprehensive access to knowledge and information and strive to constantly improve the services we provide to state government, the public and to each other.

Technology: We believe libraries must be active partners in the development and implementation of technology to ensure that access to knowledge and information will be equitably available to all.

Continuous Improvement: We believe that continuous improvement should embrace every aspect of our work and encourage our employees to look for and find ways to contribute to our development. Our employees' creativity, productivity and individual responsibility is encouraged and employees will be recognized and rewarded for their contributions.

#6 -- California State Library

CHAPTER 4

VISIONS

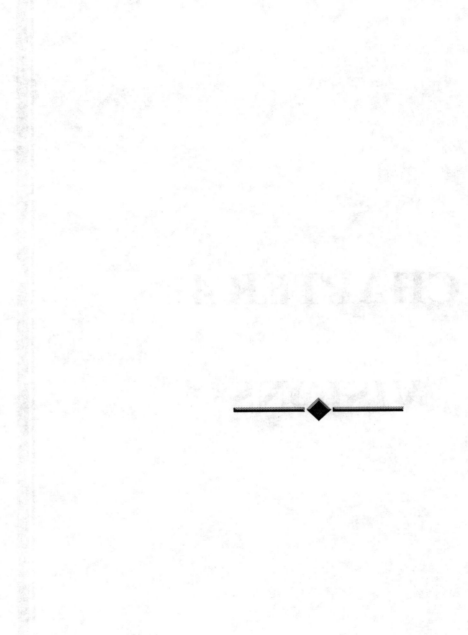

VISIONS

The process of building a common vision and working toward that vision is the essence of strategic planning. Creating an image of what the organization will look like three to five years in the future can provide a framework for moving toward this articulated ideal. An effectively used vision statement can bring inspiration and unity to the organization and can provide the bedrock of the entire plan. While the complexities of most library cooperative organizations can make the process of developing a vision statement very challenging, this same complexity makes it even more important. The decision making structure of library cooperatives and systems is typically complex and serves the interest of a diverse group of stakeholders. This diversity can uncover divergent viewpoints which need to be addressed concerning the organization's vision.

While there may be difficulties in the visioning process, the potential benefits are many:
- Members and staff of the cooperative can see the "big picture" and not be limited by their framework of day-to-day operations or current service offerings.
- By describing the future and the image of a successful organization functioning in new ways, the pathway can become clearer.
- Decision making may become more efficient as potential actions are tested against the vision.
- Conflict may be reduced if consensus has been achieved on a vision.
- The vision statement can provide motivation and inspiration to members and staff alike.

In terms of format, the submitted vision statements ranged from a single short phrase to the extended articulation of an environmental forecast along with the vision for the organization's ideal interaction and enhancement of their constituents within that ideal. In some cases, very specific statements of where the organization will be providing which services and specific system components are formulated as part of the vision for the future.

In reviewing the submitted vision statements, it was interesting to note the parallels between vision and mission statements. The vision often becomes the all encompassing job of accomplishing the mission. In other cases, past successes are cited as prelude or justification for the articulated vision. Two important themes emerge: (1) the recognition of the rapidly changing environment in which all libraries are attempting to function and (2) the diverse visions that the cooperative organizations have for their place in the new realities. These are clearly times that require creative visioning in order to position libraries and their cooperative organizations for their futures.

35

VISION AND MISSION

In 1991, the South Central Research Library Council adopted the following visions and mission. It continues to be an effective tool for focusing the work of the organization. The Strategic Plan flows from the mission statement.

> The South Central Research Library Council affirms that equal opportunity to participate in our country's economic, political and social life depends upon equal access to information; and the South Central Research Library Council affirms that libraries and library systems are the most appropriate means for ensuring this access.
>
> In carrying out that vision, the mission of the South Central Research Library Council is:

1. To connect members with each other and thus stimulate cooperation; to provide gateways into information networks.

2. To challenge members to achieve excellence and to embrace innovation so that they can flourish within an ever-changing environment.

3. To champion libraries and information services; to act as an advocate for members
   #48 -- South Central Research Library Council

VISION STATEMENT

Vision is the description of Region V's desired future impact. The vision of success for Region V is:

- ALL USERS HAVE IMPROVED ACCESS TO INFORMATION AND READING MATERIALS

- ALL LIBRARIES ARE EFFECTIVELY ABLE TO MEET THE INFORMATION AND READING NEEDS OF THEIR PATRONS

- ALL LIBRARIES BELONG, PARTICIPATE, AND CONTRIBUTE THEIR UNIQUENESS
  #10 b. -- Central Jersey Regional Library Cooperative

OUR VISION

SEFLIN member libraries are committed to working cooperatively and using the SEFLIN organization to assist libraries in meeting their individual service missions.

SEFLIN will position SEFLIN libraries as major leaders in the information structure of Southeast Florida by working cooperatively with libraries, educational institutions, information agencies, area businesses and government agencies. SEFLIN will enable libraries to transcend political boundaries and empower people to receive the information they need when they need it. SEFLIN libraries will affirm the social value of libraries as key contributors to the community's social and economic well-being and quality of life. SEFLIN libraries will facilitate the joint use of technology to provide the residents of Southeast Florida with links to local, state, regional, and global information resources.

To accomplish this, SEFLIN will remain a cooperative membership organization that provides an organizational structure that facilitates:

- the delivery of a wide range of services to meet specific regional needs;
- sharing of traditional library materials and electronic information resources;
- continuing education and training of library staff to accommodate changing roles and technological advances;
- leadership and advocacy for the advancement of libraries;
- experimentation and innovation with new technologies designed to improve the delivery of library service.

#50 b. -- Southeast Florida Library Information Network, Inc.
(Summary)

VISION STATEMENT

"Enabling member libraries to provide universal access"

#53 -- Southwest Area Multi-County Multi-Type Interlibrary Exchange

Vision Statement

The Southeast Library System envisions a world where libraries and individuals have direct and equal access to the diverse resources needed for education, work, and leisure. Technological developments will continue to challenge us to help libraries keep pace with the changing role of our profession.

#51 -- Southeast Nebraska Library System

VISION STATEMENT

We see ourselves becoming...

A public library cooperative with strong links to multi-type libraries, providing support to members through a cost effective variety of shared services, with a strong emphasis on planning and implementing technology to facilitate local services and cooperation among libraries and providing ongoing education of the value and use of libraries.

#4 -- Black Gold Cooperative Library System

VISION

The South Carolina State Library is a major leader in the planning and implementation of effective informational and library services for the people of South Carolina. It is a vital component of the State's information infrastructure.

#47 -- South Carolina State Library

Vision Statement

**If a nation expects to be ignorant and free,
in a state of civilization,
it expects what never was and never will be.**
Thomas Jefferson

We live in a society where information has become one of the most important commodities for personal and business success. Further, our form of government is based on the premise that the voters must remain informed about important issues in order to make wise decisions and guard the rights of all citizens. It has become increasingly difficult for the individual to cope with the pressures of the burgeoning amount of information, the bewildering array of new technologies designed to access information, and the financial resources required to acquire technology. The result is a growing division of society into the information "have" and "have-nots."

The Central Florida Library Consortium envisions itself as an equalizer of access to information and a pathfinder in assisting users to navigate the expanding information highway. It is dedicated to making information available to all citizens of Central Florida, regardless of user affiliation or economic circumstances, through a seamless interface to the network of information resources by coordinating the efforts of its member libraries to identify and share resources, by providing continuing education opportunities for the staff and users of member libraries, and by serving as a central focus for exploring new technologies, resources and methods of accessing information at the local, state, national, and international levels.

#9 -- Central Florida Library Cooperative

PROJECT OVERVIEW

In 1986, when the first Florida Resource Sharing Plan was written, the Network Planning Committee adopted the library networking common vision of the Library of Congress Network Advisory Committee. The Network Planning Task Force reviewed this mission statement and agreed that the statement still reflected the vision of networking in Florida.

(From the Library of Congress Network of Advisory Committee's "Library Networking": A Statement of a Common Vision")

Our common vision of networking is an environment in which libraries can provide each individual in the United States with equal opportunity of access to resources that will satisfy their and society's information needs and interests. All users should have access on a timely basis to the information they require without being faced with costs beyond their own or society's means.

To realize this vision, there must be technical and intellectual sharing of resources between the public and private sectors; local, state, and federal governments must fulfill their various responsibilities to individuals and society; and the diverse missions of the several types of libraries must be accommodated. As this vision becomes a reality, there will emerge a diverse but coordinated structure of networks rather than a monolithic one. Active research, rapidly developing technology, collaborative leadership, common standards, and shared communications will provide means by which the system will be further shaped as an interlocking series of local, state, regional, national, and international relationships that are capable of serving the national's information needs.

In Florida, as well as nationally, there is a paradigm shift occurring within libraries. Increasingly, the information necessary to respond to user information needs is available electronically... sometimes only electronically and sometimes most conveniently electronically. Despite the electronic revolution sweeping the country, many people still do not have the knowledge or ability to access these electronic information sources on their own. To maximize the use of these resources, people need help. The library is both the most appropriate and the best place to help people get the information they want.

The new electronic information environment allows librarians to substantially augment the services of libraries. This electronic environment allows libraries to access additional information resources previously unavailable, to deliver information and documents in more convenient and efficient ways, and to provide new services previously not possible or feasible. Librarians must be knowledgeable about these new opportunities and have the equipment and training to access electronic information when it improves the libraries ability to serve its users.

#17 -- Florida Network Planning Task Force and the State Library of Florida

A VISION FOR KDLA

A dynamic, evolving organization, the Kentucky Department for Libraries and Archives is a leader in providing quality management and delivery of information resources. It envisions a future in which:

Kentucky is a state whose people have equitable access to the information resources they need for work and home; where government policy and action is well documented and the management of public records promotes government efficiency; and where our libraries are vital partners in the development of this state.

Public libraries are an essential, vibrant element in their communities -- places where citizens have unlimited access to a wide variety of information, and are served by well-trained library and archival professionals. With government information readily accessible to citizens, all public agencies are partners with KDLA in meeting documentation and records management responsibilities and have active, ongoing records management programs.

KDLA has forged productive partnerships with these citizens and public agencies, and is known for its staff's strong service orientation, its ability to access a wealth of information resources, and its effective use of technology in all aspects of its work.

#23 -- Kentucky Department for Libraries & Archives

THE VISION
**All citizens of New Jersey participate fully and share
equitably in the benefits of the information revolution.**

Every New Jersey library has the necessary resources to access the world of information.
Every New Jersey citizen has access to information about the local, state and federal government through library technology.
Every New Jersey citizen can communicate electronically with government officials.
Every New Jersey citizen can receive training and support at their local library in accessing, evaluating and using electronic information.
Every New Jersey citizen has access to information 24 hours a day. This access may be from home, school, office, library and other public places.

#36 -- New Jersey State Library

The Vision

In the year 2000, the South Dakota Library Network (SDLN) will reach into every school, public, academic, and special library, and into every state and local government office in South Dakota. Electronic gateways will provide access by businesses and community organizations to SDLN. Network databases will be accessed via terminals in member libraries or dial-up modems and via Internet/NTI (National Technology Infrastructure). Internet/NTI gateways will allow users of SDLN to access other library catalogs worldwide. A subsystem, to permit online reference assistance, will join subsystems already available: acquisitions, catalog, cataloging, circulation, interlibrary loan, inventory control and serials. Additional databases (bibliographic, full-text, and multimedia) will be added to the options available on the online catalog. Shared collection development information will enable member libraries to maximize resource expenditures. Improved hardware and software will lead to the inclusion of digital audio and video image technology. SDLN will be linked using the high-speed fiberoptic backbone of state, regional, and federal telecommunication networks.

As community networks evolve, SDLN will be utilized by people at home and on the move via computers, sophisticated televisions, and smart phones to create an information environment. This environment will supply needed information and will engage people in learning. When fully evolved, this information environment will exist on many levels, be multi-sensory, multi-modal, and capable of being personalized to the individual, to curriculums, or to business needs. In this environment, the library world will be part of a virtual world where learning is accomplished via simulation.

The South Dakota Library Network is both a backbone and a beginning to support the information services that will be demanded by the citizens of South Dakota in the future.

#49 -- South Dakota State Library

The State Advisory Council on Libraries Challenge

The State Advisory Council on Libraries challenges Nebraska Libraries to link every citizen of the state with information technologies by becoming a catalyst for community planning and aggressively obtaining funding. Libraries are challenged to partner to accomplish the goal of information access. Librarians are challenged to increase their knowledge and ability to use information technologies to serve their communities.

#32 -- Nebraska Library Commission

Vision of the Council of Wisconsin Libraries

The combined resources of the libraries in Wisconsin are accessible and available to the people of Wisconsin; that is, every library, regardless of location in the State, size of facility, or type of institution, is a gateway for its users to the entire Wisconsin library community. Any library user can easily search the collective resources; can determine the current availability of specific information; and, subject to the holding library's policies, may obtain materials and/or information from any of the library resources within the State in a timely and economical fashion. The people of Wisconsin are made aware of these services and are encouraged to use them.

ACHIEVING THE VISION: <u>THE ROLE OF COWL & SETTING GOALS</u>

If the vision of information access and resource sharing is to be realized, it will be done through an evolutionary process requiring the concentrated attention of the entire Wisconsin library community. Wisconsin libraries must begin to think of resource sharing in a broader context. That is, the definition of resource sharing must be expanded to include sharing of electronic resources and sharing of information and reference services as well as traditional interlibrary loan. Planning must encompass the issues of access to materials and information (identifying, locating and requesting what is to be shared), issues of delivery (how to move materials and information from the owning library to the patron), issues of funding (how does the library community as a whole assure financial equity), and issues of the library role in emerging new technologies. It will also require enhancing the public image of libraries as an essential interface between people and information.

#15 -- Council of Wisconsin Libraries, Inc.

PRIORITY # 1

Create a statewide community of strong libraries working together to achieve Vision 2004.

Libraries must rely on cooperation and networking of all material, staff, and electronic resources to meet the information needs of North Dakota citizens in order to face the growing challenges of global interdependence and global competition; the ever-increasing information explosion; the continuing evolution in computer and communications technologies; and the increased need for lifelong learning, job retraining, and recreation.

#39 -- North Dakota State Library

Our Vision

The California State Library will be the most dynamic state library in the nation and will be recognized as such.

#6 -- California State Library

VISION STATEMENT

The Alliance vision is to establish itself as a state, regional and national leadership organization by augmenting and enhancing initiatives taken by members through the innovative use of systems and technology. Characteristics of leadership include:

- Vision
- Visibility
- Articulation
- Leveraging investments
- Working in high impact arenas
- Collaboration on overhead
- Risk Taking
- Bias for Action

This Strategic Plan represents a major change of direction for the Alliance. With the evolution of the Alliance into a multi-vendor-based consortium, the new emphasis is on the cooperative development of a nationally recognized electronic library to benefit local patrons of the member institutions.

#13 -- Colorado Alliance of Research Libraries

VISION STATEMENT

PALINET leads libraries in shaping tomorrow for themselves and their customers. PALINET is entrepreneurial, member supportive and a key source of technical expertise.

Vision is a futuristic picture of the organization. This vision statement demands that PALINET exercise leadership in helping libraries to shape their tomorrows, not be shaped by them. It indicates that PALINET must be an agile organization, able to capitalize on opportunities as they arise and to maintain the technical expertise necessary to do so, while maintaining a strong orientation to ongoing service and support of its members and customers.

#43 -- PALINET

The Vision for Change.

SOLINET will establish itself as a major force in the information infrastructure of the Southeast. Working with libraries, archives, educational and information agencies, and business and public policy organizations, SOLINET will contribute to the economic development, educational enhancement, and overall quality of life in the region.

To accomplish this, SOLINET will remain a cooperative membership organization that provides the structure to support:

- A wide range of services designed to meet specific regional needs and to enable members to accomplish that which they can do better collectively.

- An expanded leadership role, representing libraries and archives, to bring about change through education and to assist in the development of public information policy .

- Equitable access to information for the citizens of the Southeast.

- The training and education of library and archives staff in response to changing roles and technological advances.

- Connectivity among institutions in the Southeast through telecommunications, publications, conferences, and the establishment of resource sharing groups.

- A bridging function to encourage cooperation among business, industry, government, and information agencies.

- Shared research and development efforts of various groups of libraries and archives in the region.

- Ongoing commitment to the development of SOLINET staff expertise and quality in support of southeastern library programs and needs.

- Diversity in sources of revenue, resulting in financial strength for SOLINET and cost containment for its members.

 # 52 -- SOLINET (Southeastern Library Network inc.)

CRL was founded in 1949 by ten midwestern universities and research libraries to improve access to increasing numbers of foreign research publications and to assist member libraries in reducing the processing, storage and delivery costs associated with rarely-held, but vital, collections. Since then, CRL has operated cooperative collection development programs based on its large managed, centralized collection categorized primarily by format of material and area of the world. These programs have allowed member libraries to concentrate on building their core and special collections as CRL has taken responsibility for many peripheral and supplementary materials.

The CRL of tomorrow will continue to advance and serve scholarship, especially academic research, which requires access to both core and peripheral collections that are global as well as domestic resources. Increasingly, research libraries need sound cooperative mechanisms for effectively placing resources into the hands of users when they want them. CRL, with an important collection of global research materials and as an established and successful framework for interlibrary cooperation, will use its singular position to maximize its value and relevance to the library and information communities.

CRL will focus on programs that rely on cost sharing and saving for research libraries. CRL will build on existing strengths while reaching out toward new challenges and opportunities. An ongoing commitment to maintain the scope of current collecting activities will continue to be a high priority for CRL, which will offer ongoing access to rarely held and valuable research materials in a collection dedicated to supplementing local holdings. Simultaneously, CRL will develop new collecting policies and procedures for research materials published in electronic format. As a collection of both first and last resort, CRL places great importance on the preservation of library materials and on the use of digital technology to integrate the preserving, storing, and delivering of materials now in paper and film.

CRL will seek out opportunities for greater international collaboration among libraries, establishing alliances and partnerships arising from existing frameworks and will seek out new ventures that will enhance its programs. CRL offers an excellent operational testing ground for collaborative projects, and can serve as an opportunity for the information producing and using communities to come together and work out fresh patterns of interaction and exchange. CRL's dual attributes as both a broad-based cooperative organization and a major research library, afford an ideal venue for implementing creative strategies. CRL is an organization able to function successfully as both facilitator and coordinator in the changing dynamics of the evolving information environment.

CRL will continue to be an organization driven by programs supportable by financial resources that are economically feasible to sustain over the long term. CRL will develop new revenue streams, chiefly program services and grantsmanship, to support growth in core operations and special projects, respectively. This will have the effect of reducing the rate of rise of membership fees.

CRL will insure that access to its growing collections is available in a format and medium that efficiently serves the needs of scholars both now and in the future. This will require an enduring commitment to Internet compatibility, including users directly searching, requesting, and receiving CRL collections. The World Wide Web will become a primary vehicle for publishing and distributing an expanding variety of materials to an increasingly larger user community worldwide.

#7 -- Center for Research Libraries

CHAPTER 5

MISSIONS

MISSION

A library cooperative must be clear about why it exists. The core underlying purposes of the organization are articulated in its mission statement. It needs to be understood and agreed upon by all of its stakeholders, the Board, the staff and the members. Without this common understanding of the fundamental mission of the organization, effective planning and program development is unlikely to take place. The careful formulation or reformulation of the organization's mission statement obviously needs to be among the first major steps in the strategic planning process.

A well developed mission statement provides a number of benefits both to the planning process and to organizational success. These include:
- a focus for the "business" of the organization which allows a course-setting framework for all strategies and activities,
- a context for tying resource allocations to the critical strategies for meeting mission priorities,
- a clear statement of the organization's purpose for potential partners and funding agencies,
- a decision tool for program and project strategies.

In the review of submitted planning documents, it was interesting to note that mission statements ranged from a short sentence to fairly long lists. They ranged from very broad statements of function to specific identifications of the targeted clientele with generic descriptions of the kinds of services and/or products to be provided by the organization. In several cases, the planning team included *their definition* of a mission statement in their presentation of the organization's mission statement.

In terms of commonalties, almost all of the submitted statements attempt to describe, usually clearly and concisely, the core purpose and enterprise of the organization. Each provokes the logical next question -- How are we going to do this? -- which sets the stage for the strategic approach to planning. Some of the specific elements of the submitted mission statements include: enhancing access, facilitating cooperative programs and partnerships, meeting the community's need to know, and providing advocacy for libraries. Strengthening member libraries or enabling libraries to improve services are also recurring themes in the following mission statements. Emphasis on these improvements to benefit the end user community is often stated or implied.

MISSION STATEMENT

The mission of Region V is to:

BRING LIBRARIES TOGETHER. REGION V PROMOTES COOPERATION AND FACILITATES THE EFFECTIVE SHARING OF RESOURCES, INFORMATION AND SERVICES.

The mission and vision of Region V flow from its purpose. Mission defines "what business the Region is in order to achieve its purpose." It incorporates the primary methods by which the Region will achieve its purpose and the underlying assumptions, beliefs, and philosophy which inform the Region's purpose and programs.

Library service in Region V has been and continues to be uneven. Funding levels vary and all are limited by a tight economy. Both small and large libraries feel constrained in terms of personnel and collection development. Advances in technology are so rapid and costly that even large libraries find it difficult to keep current.

At the same time, demand for library service is growing in quantity and quality. It is the Committee's assumption that no library -- school, public, special or academic -- can satisfy all of their patrons' needs all of the time.

The Region provides the opportunity for access to resources through a comprehensive array of programs and services, and it has a responsibility to assist member libraries in identifying which services are most useful to them.

PURPOSE STATEMENT

The purpose of Region V is to:

STRENGTHEN MEMBER LIBRARIES' ABILITY TO MEET PATRONS' NEEDS

Establishing a clear single sentence purpose statement is the foundation for the development of a successful strategic plan. The Committee asked, "Why does the Region exist and what do we want it to accomplish?"

Discussion focused on improving patron access to resources and information but also addressed the differences between member libraries in terms of mission, funding, size of collection, access to information, and ability to share resources.

The Committee realized that the purpose must focus on member libraries who in turn will provide service to patrons. The purpose statement establishes the ultimate result for which Region V exists and will focus the Region's planning and resources during the next five years.

#10 b. -- Central Jersey Regional Library Cooperative

The Mission of SOLINET

The mission of the Southeastern Library Network, Inc. (SOLINET), a diversified, not-for profit membership organization, is to offer services and products that enable members and their constituents to employ, primarily through resource sharing and development, the most effective and economical means available in rendering library and other information services for the educational, cultural, research, and economic advancement of the Southeast.

#52 -- SOLINET (Southeastern Library Network Inc.)

MOLO's Mission Statement:

As a basic tenet, the MOLO Board of Trustees agreed that MOLO's focus should be toward developing and supporting roles which serve the library institutions, administrators, trustees, and staffs. The Board agreed that MOLO programs serving patrons directly confuses the role MOLO plays with regard to its membership and also sets up a "competitive" or redundant service with local libraries. Therefore MOLO's mission statement has been changed from: ***Cooperating to extend and enhance service to our member libraries' users*** to
Cooperating to enhance our member's library services to their users.

#31 -- MOLO Regional Library System

The Southwest Regional Library Service System, hereinafter known as "SWRLSS" (pronounced "swirls") has adopted as its mission: **to strengthen, support and equalize member library services by providing leadership and encouraging cooperation among libraries in order to improve public access to information**.

#54 -- Southwest Regional Library Services System

MISSION STATEMENT:

The North Country Reference and Research Resources Council is a regional multitype library agency primarily dedicated to cooperatively providing support and services necessary for all of its members to meet their individual goals. The Council serves libraries in the seven counties of Northern New York for the ultimate benefit of the library user.

#38 -- North Country Reference & Research Resources Council

OUR MISSION

SEFLIN, a non-profit membership organization of Southeast Florida libraries, believes that libraries can make a difference in people's lives. Our mission is to work cooperatively with our members and the community to promote the collection and sharing of library resources, to facilitate training, to increase public awareness, to provide leadership, to encourage the joint use of technology and to support activities that enhance an individual library's ability to meet the informational, educational and cultural needs of its primary users and Southeast Florida residents.

#50 b. -- Southeast Florida Library Information Network, Inc.
(Summary)

MISSION
The South Carolina State Library's mission is to improve library services throughout the state and to ensure all citizens access to libraries and information resources adequate to meet their needs. The State Library supports libraries in meeting the informational, educational, cultural, and recreational needs of the people of South Carolina.

#47 -- South Carolina State Library

Mission Statement

The Southeast Library System works proactively with library personnel and with other agencies to help them meet the diverse informational needs of their patrons. Innovative, interdependent and seamless approaches will be used to provide services.

#51 -- Southeast Nebraska Library System

Lakeland Library Cooperative strengthens member libraries in eight west Michigan counties by providing the means to share resources, services and expertise for the benefit of individuals and communities.

#24 -- Lakeland Library Cooperative

The Mission

The South Dakota Library Network provides all residents of South Dakota with rapid, easy access to the information, materials, and services of its member libraries.

#49 -- South Dakota State Library

Mission Statement: Acknowledging the ever increasing interdependence of all types of libraries, the Meridian Library System will focus on those activities that best support, serve and promote the individual strengths of its constituents. It will be innovative, proactive and stress those activities and services necessary to accomplish system goals which include consulting, resource sharing and provision of continuing education activities.

#28 -- Meridian Library System

MISSION STATEMENT

The Bergen County Cooperative Library System is a federation of public libraries that promotes high quality library service to the general public through resource sharing. Reciprocal borrowing among its member libraries is the cornerstone program of the organization.

BCCLS derives its strength from its synergistic nature while maintaining respect for each library's autonomy.

BCCLS initiates, nurtures and manages cooperative public library programs and services which provide their users the widest possible access to all types of library materials and information.

BCCLS facilitates the role of public libraries in a global technologically based community.

BCCLS encourages libraries as community centers in meeting the intellectual, cultural, and recreational needs of individuals, families, groups, and businesses.

BCCLS upholds the principle that professional reference and information services should be available to the members of BCCLS and all residents of Bergen County.

BCCLS supports coalition and consensus building as key steps to successfully address library needs at the local, county, state, and national levels for both adequate funding and appropriate legislation.

BCCLS believes that its libraries are enhanced by the open exchange of ideas and resources through formal and informal means as well as professional activities.

BCCLS affirms that libraries are forums for information and ideas and endorses the ALA Library Bill of Rights.

#2 -- Bergen County Cooperative Library System

MISSION STATEMENT

The N.H. Automated Information System will provide the residents of New Hampshire rapid access to library and informational resources through a coordinated statewide information network.

#35 -- New Hampshire State Library

MISSION STATEMENT

The mission of PALINET is to assist staff of libraries and information centers to deliver high quality, cost-effective services to their users through the application of technologies that foster information access, resource sharing and interlibrary cooperation

Mission *describes the contribution of the organization to achievement of the vision in a precise, concise and inspiring declaration of the fundamental purpose for which the organization exists. This mission statement establishes the long-range view of the organization's role in the library and information marketplace and provides the framework within which goals and objectives are defined.*

#43 -- PALINET

BCR'S MISSION STATEMENT
The Bibliographical Center for Research (BCR) is organized as a not-for-profit corporation to assist in the effective and economical delivery of high-quality library and information services. BCR operations serve the membership by helping the library community to share information resources, by providing access to information services, by developing and promoting new technologies for information organization and delivery and by carrying out training and technical assistance in the use of information services. BCR encourages and assists communication among the members and serves as their advocate on regional and national library and information issues.

#3 -- Bibliographical Center for Research, Rocky Mountain Region, Inc.

Our Mission
The mission of AMIGOS is to:
Provide innovative information services,
Promote regional cooperation and resource-sharing, and
Support libraries as leaders in education and information services.

#1 -- AMIGOS

Mission
The mission of the Connecticut State Library is to provide high quality library and information services to state government and the citizens of Connecticut; to work cooperatively with related agencies and constituent organizations in providing those services; to preserve and make available the records of Connecticut's history and heritage; to promote the development and growth of high quality information services on an equitable basis statewide; to provide leadership and cooperative opportunities for the library, educational, and historical communities in order to enhance the value of their individual and collective service missions; and to develop and promote appropriate legislation and public policy in support of these efforts.

#14 -- Connecticut State Library

MISSION
The mission of the Nebraska Library Commission is statewide promotion, development, and coordination of library and information services. As the state library agency, the Commission is an advocate for the library and information service needs of all Nebraskans.

#32 -- Nebraska Library Commission

MISSION
The Colorado Alliance of Research Libraries is a partnership of research, public and educational institutions working in concert to serve the information needs of the constituencies of member institutions and the general public. The two fold mission of the Alliance is: 1) to share resources, and 2) to identify and solve problems of information creation, collection, access and distribution. The Alliance institutions seek to reduce member operating costs and provide additional services to its constituencies by sharing their resources, expertise and leveraged purchasing. In pursuit of its mission the Alliance will:

- Offer automated and conventional systems or cooperative arrangements to enhance access to information resources
- Forge alliances with other organizations that offer information products and services
- Share ideas and strategies for managing changing conditions in the library environment
- Sponsor research which seeks solutions to a wide range of information management problems
- Develop strategies for reducing costs.

#13 -- Colorado Alliance of Research Libraries

MISSION STATEMENT

DEFINITION: An organization's mission should provide a general description of its fundamental and global reason for being. It should be brief, clear, and broad enough to allow flexibility in implementation. An effective mission is a means by which managers and others can make decisions; reflect the values, beliefs, philosophy, and culture of the organization; and serve as an energy source and rallying point for the organization.

*****

The Kentucky Department for Libraries and Archives serves Kentucky's need to know by assuring equitable access to high quality library and information resources and services and by helping public agencies ensure that adequate documentation of government programs is created, efficiently maintained and made readily accessible.

#23 -- Kentucky Department for Libraries & Archives

The Network Mission:

A key starting point of the planning process was the crafting of a new mission statement that would refocus the network and its member institutions on their basic reason for existence: The improvement of services to library and information users. The New Network Mission Statement is:

The Network assures that all Indiana residents receive the best possible library and information services by providing a cooperative, statewide structure for information and resource sharing.

#21 -- Indiana State Library

VISION AND MISSION

In 1991, the South Central Research Library Council adopted the following vision and mission. It continues to be an effective tool for focusing the work of the organization. The Strategic Plan flows from the mission statement.

The South Central Research Library Council affirms that equal opportunity to participate in our country's economic, political and social life depends upon equal access to information; and the South Central Research Library Council affirms that libraries and library systems are the most appropriate means for ensuring this access.

In carrying out that vision, the mission of the South Central Research Library Council is:

1. To connect members with each other and thus stimulate cooperation; to provide gateways into information networks.
2. To challenge members to achieve excellence and to embrace innovation so that they can flourish within an ever-changing environment.
3. To champion libraries and information services; to act as an advocate for members.

#48 -- South Central Research Library Council

CHAPTER 6

ENVIRONMENTAL ANALYSIS

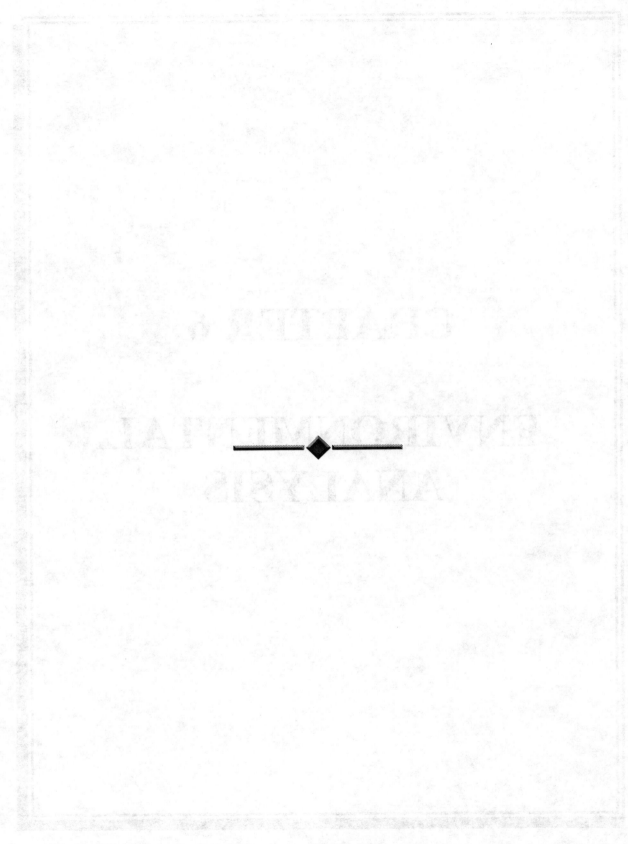

ENVIRONMENTAL ANALYSIS

An on-going awareness of what is happening in both the internal and external environments is essential to an organization's future. Responding effectively to changes in the environment, positions an organization strategically. This environmental awareness is especially critical during the planning process. Making the commitment to the hard work associated with completing the environmental scan can pay off in many ways for the strategic planning effort. Among the more important are:

- an understanding by all members of the planning team of the organization's history, how it is financed, membership issues and patterns of usage of services,
- a "reality check" on the external threats to the organization's future including changing funding priorities of granting agencies, commercial service offerings and multiple layers of library cooperatives and networks,
- a firm basis and context for thinking strategically, rather than simply building incrementally on current operations or status quo.

There are many different ways to study and process the environmental influences. Broad environmental trends including technological factors, economic trends, political factors and social patterns can be gathered from the literature and from a commitment to staying current. For example, trends such as the increasing reliance upon distance education can have major effects upon the environment of the library cooperative.

The primary method for presenting the outcome of this process among the submitted planning documents is to formulate segmented listings. The traditional SWOT analysis is present, as well as, other innovative ways of characterizing the elements such as: identifying key trends, paradigm shifts, membership issues and drawing assumptions about the environmental context. The traditional review of strengths and weaknesses, opportunities and threats (SWOT) can be a very revealing part of the planning effort for a library cooperative or system. It can also be very difficult to maintain an objective viewpoint during a SWOT analysis. Garnering member input can be a critical part of the process since members' perceptions of staff and services are difficult to objectively evaluate during daily operations and governance. Survey results can also aid in this portion of the environmental scan.

A review of the submitted plans revealed the major influence which the information technology revolution is having upon library cooperatives and systems. Issues associated with traditional resource sharing technologies are rare. Issues dealing with document delivery, re-defining library services, new roles in information management and delivery, and partnership opportunities are emerging. The uncertainties of database licensing and redefining copyright are recurring issues and opportunities for library systems and cooperatives. Of course, financial issues are commonly cited in the environmental scan.

THE PLANNING ENVIRONMENT: STRATEGIC RESPONSES

The Task Force recognized that long-range planning, indeed any activity, takes place within an external, operating environment that influences the outcome of an endeavor. The environment is usually an admixture of elements that are at once supportive, neutral and inhospitable to accomplishing a plan's goals and objectives. Accordingly, this section of the Technology Plan identifies both environmental issues impinging on the Plan itself and strategic responses to those issues which represent the context within which the plan is carried forward. Certain responses may appear to resemble goals, objectives or actions in the Plan, while others "simply" reflect the need for a continuing sense of awareness and recognition. The Cooperative must decide how best to proceed with implementing the Plan while simultaneously responding to the environmental issues and pressures that impinge upon it. . . .

The Task Force distinguished five issue areas and a series of responses by the Cooperative to each of them, which are presented here as follows:

Issue 1:   Technology as Opportunity
The ubiquitous presence of technology in our society and its pervasive influence upon our profession are the reasons why there is a need for this Plan in the first place. Technology represents an open door, one through which we are invited to pass, improving and building upon the tools we employ to satisfy the informational and educational needs of the people and institutions we serve.

Strategic responses include:

1. Continuing to seek opportunities for networking our libraries, on the assumption that none of us can provide everything on our own and technology provides the alternative for trying to do so.

2. As an integral part of the above, placing an emphasis on the inter-connectivity of systems between and among our libraries.

3. Facilitating access to unique information resources that heretofore did not exist (e.g. Internet discussion groups) or were usually inaccessible (e.g. technical reports of governmental or quasi-governmental agencies.)

4. Strengthening the ability of librarians to act as navigators for a population.
                                 #10 a. -- Central Jersey Regional Library Cooperative

ENVIRONMENTAL ISSUES

The Task Force identified the following issues as the most important issues which could affect the South Central Research Library Council in the next few years.

- There is a potential for change in the nature of the organization due to:
    - lack of legislative funding increases.
    - mood of change at the State Education Department.
    - lack of political clout and connections.
    - ambiguous future for New York State library systems.
- The nature of library users is changing. The number of users who are sophisticated and demanding seems to be increasing, while at the same time the number of non-users of libraries also appears to be increasing.
- Corporate downsizing and the emergence of small and new businesses suggests that there will be an increase in the number and type of businesses needing information, but it may be provided outside the traditional corporate library structure.
- Growth and change in technology means that physical boundaries are less important; retraining staff and re-tooling equipment will be needed.
- Revenue is in decline and is unpredictable.
- Information is increasing in availability, formats and products.
- There will be more emphasis on measuring outcomes and accountability.
- Document delivery is now available in new forms; there is a changing attitude towards ownership vs. access.

STRENGTHS OF THE ORGANIZATION

The Task Force identified the following strengths of the South Central Research Library Council.

- The organizational infrastructure including strong advisory committees; good board of trustees; and a history of producing and delivering quality programs and services.
- The staff who take leadership positions, are innovative, risk-taking, creative.
- The ability of the organization to be a conduit for information and the connect organizations.
- The membership: its variety of resources and people, its willingness to cooperate.
- The continuing education program which has a long history of providing quality workshops for library staff.
- The organization and activity of the Library Assistants (library clerical and support staff).
- The results achieved through library automation and technology funding using state and federal funds.
- Resource sharing among members, and the document delivery subsidies which support this sharing.

WEAKNESSES

The Task Force identified the following weaknesses of the organization.
- The lack of consistent and stable funding from New York State.
- Lack of strategic alliances; ineffective lobbying strategies.
- Lack of understanding regarding the organization's purpose, mission, organizational vision.
- Decision-making processes within the organization are not clear.
- The lack of a technical infrastructure in the office, especially the restrictive access to the Internet.
- Lack of understanding among librarians working in different types of libraries regarding each other's role and value.
- Lack of a future-oriented focus for the Regional Automation Program.
- The Documentary Heritage Program, due to lack of state support and target audience which is not membership based.

MEMBERSHIP NEEDS

The most important membership needs were identified at the October 11, 1992 Annual Membership Meeting, when participants met in small groups to discuss questions regarding expected changes in members' libraries, barriers and incentives to those changes, and ideas for how South Central Research Library Council could help.
- Assistance in anticipating, planning for, and managing change.
- Development of leadership skills.
- Assistance with the advocacy role; help with promoting and marketing the library both internally and externally.
- Organizational consulting.
- More education and training.
- A format for getting together, relationship building.
- Help in staying on the leading edge of technology.
- More access points to information, better delivery of information.

#48 -- South Central Research Library Council

KEY ISSUES FACING MASSACHUSETTS LIBRARIES

Libraries have played a key role in Massachusetts' cultural and economic development for more than three hundred years. Libraries serve as a focus for intellectual growth, research and learning for people of all ages. Through libraries, cities and towns schools, institutions and businesses provide collective access to books and other resources which no individual could hope to afford.

Currently, nearly 2,800 academic, public, school, institutional and corporate libraries serve the people of the Commonwealth, and their combined collections of books and other materials constitute one of the richest intellectual resources in the nation.

Today, our society and these libraries are challenged by several major trends that are changing the way we work, learn and communicate. The first of these trends is **globalization**. Increasingly, we live and work in an environment of global interdependence and global competition where personal, educational and corporate success is determined by timely access to global information resources.

The second trend is **the information explosion**. During the last half century, published information has increased at an unprecedented rate, with the total amount of recorded information estimated to be doubling every ten to twenty years. Acquiring, organizing and making this information accessible presents a serious and growing challenge.

The third trend is the revolution in computer technology, which has created **a new world of electronic access to information**. While books and periodicals will continue to serve as the main source of information for education and communication for many generations to come, new electronic information systems are augmenting and, in many instances, replacing traditional printed information sources. This creates tremendous challenges for the individuals, businesses and institutions which must learn to use them effectively. An even more serious problem is the emerging chasm between information "haves" and "have nots." If all citizens are to meet their full economic and personal potential, they must not only be print literate, but now must be information literate as well.

The fourth trend is an acceleration in the rate of technological change which has created **an increased need for lifelong learning and retraining**. It is now estimated that today's eighteen-year-olds will change employment several times in their lives, with new skills required each time. For the first time in history, lifelong learning has become more than desirable -- it has become an economic necessity.

Today, the Commonwealth's businesses and workers are trying to cope with staggering growth in publication, information and human knowledge while learning how to compete in an information-driven global economy that requires access to global information resources. The Massachusetts economy has always depended heavily on the informational resources acquired, organized, and maintained by libraries. It would be extremely short-sighted to believe that Massachusetts will be able to compete in the emerging information-based economy without continued access to strong libraries and the new electronic information resources.

As we enter the 21st century, libraries must continue to serve as intellectual and cultural centers for their communities by maintaining strong collections of books and periodicals. At the same time, they must also provide access to an expanding world of information and keep pace with changes in information technology. It is clear that libraries can and will plan a critical role in preparing Massachusetts residents to meet the challenges of the future, but their ability to do so effectively will be determined by the following key issues:

KEY ISSUE 1: The End of the Stand-Alone Library

Half a century ago, a well-funded academic, public, school, institutional or corporate library could reasonably expect to meet most of the needs of its users through a collection of materials housed within a single building. Since that time, the rapid growth in publishing and the accompanying dramatic increases in the variety and specialization of user needs have far outstripped the capacity of any library. During the last decade, however, library funding has failed to keep pace with these growing needs due to the combined effect of inflation and local budget cuts.

Libraries have responded to the crisis of increasing demands and limited resources through a greater reliance on regionalization, cooperation and networking. Two major State initiatives in this area include the Regional Public Library Systems and the automated resource sharing networks, both of which provide libraries with expanded access to materials and information not available locally. However, the state supported regional library systems generally serve public libraries only, and while some of the automated resource sharing networks are multitype, they serve only one-tenth of all libraries in the Commonwealth. What is needed is a statewide structure to effectively link existing programs and extend the benefits of regionalization, cooperation, and networking to all libraries.

KEY ISSUE 2: The Need for Closer Cooperation Among Different Types of Libraries

As individual libraries increasingly rely on cooperation and networking, it has become clear that libraries of all types need to work together much more closely if they are to meet all the information needs of users. Currently, most Massachusetts public libraries find it easier to locate information on materials in another public library across the state than in a school library across the street.

Massachusetts residents use different libraries throughout their lives. They use public libraries as preschoolers, as students, as parents, as workers, and as lifelong learners. They use school and academic libraries as students, and institutional and corporate libraries as workers. If libraries are to meet the rapidly changing needs of residents in the future, they must have cooperative structures which allow them to connect users with the widest range of possible resources, regardless of which type of library provides this connection.

KEY ISSUE 3: The Need for a Statewide Structure for Cooperation and Access

Cooperation allows individual libraries to serve their users more effectively by offering them access to the resources of other libraries, but state support is required to make the full range of resources available to residents.

Since 1960, the Commonwealth has supported limited cooperation between public libraries on a regional level, including some support for shared automated networks, and since 1970 has provided support for the maintenance of a research collection accessible to all residents. What is needed beyond these successful programs is an overall structure to promote cooperation and improved access to information among all libraries on a statewide basis.

State-supported programs for cooperation and networking among different types of libraries are currently in place in almost every other state, and are particularly well developed in states with technology-oriented economies. Without such a program, the Commonwealth is at a severe competitive disadvantage. While Massachusetts libraries hold a wealth of resources, access to many specialized resources of statewide importance is limited or nonexistent. A statewide structure for cooperation would make more of these specialized resources accessible through libraries to businesses and individuals who do not currently have ready access to them.

Massachusetts is also fortunate to possess a unique strength: the unusually rich and varied library resources of private institutions. To take full advantage of this asset, the resources of these libraries should be made more accessible. To do this while also addressing the unequal burden which resource sharing can place on larger or stronger libraries of all types, it is critical that statewide mechanisms are created to ensure that no disproportionate burden of participation is placed on any library or group of libraries without appropriate compensation.

KEY ISSUE 4: Inequities in Access to Information
Currently, the quality and range of services offered by individual academic, public, school, institutional and corporate libraries varies from excellent to totally inadequate. Approximately one-fourth of all public libraries do not even meet minimum standards for library service, and many school libraries in the Commonwealth rank among the most poorly supported in the nation. Further serious inequities exist in the rural sections of the Commonwealth and in urban areas. To help address these inequities, a commitment must be made by the Commonwealth, as it has already been made by most other states, to guarantee that every resident has a basic level of access to information.

A basic level of access to electronic information can be made available in every library throughout the Commonwealth at relatively low cost if provided on a statewide basis. Without this basic access, millions of residents will not have the information they need to achieve their personal and economic potential.

KEY ISSUE 5: The Need for a Statewide Electronic Information Network
During the last two decades, advances in computer technology have stimulated dramatic growth in the number and variety of electronic information sources. As traditional printed catalogs are being replaced by computerized catalogs, many traditional reference sources and periodicals are being replaced by computerized databases. The impact of this growing world of electronic information is being felt in every library throughout the Commonwealth, along with strong growth in demand for electronic information services -- a demand libraries are at present largely unable to meet.

Statewide access to computerized information requires an "information highway" which will link libraries and library users with online electronic information sources. Initiatives at the national level (the National Research and Education Network, or NREN) and the New England regional level provide the backbone telecommunications system (known collectively as the Internet) necessary for the provision of electronic information resources to libraries. However, a statewide network linking all libraries to these regional and national networks is essential in order to provide Massachusetts residents with the full range of electronic information resources. The current program of state support for telecommunications linkages among libraries currently reaches only 250 of the nearly 2,800 libraries in the Commonwealth.

KEY ISSUE 6: The Challenge of Learning How to Use the New Information Technologies
While new computer and telecommunications technologies offer exciting possibilities for students, businesses and researchers, the people of the Commonwealth cannot fully utilize these electronic information systems unless they are print, computer and information literate.

End users of these new electronic information systems will require considerable assistance and training. These users will also need knowledgeable librarians to assist them in locating information and learning new skills. User education must begin in public libraries with preschool children (when critical learning patterns are set) and continue through elementary and secondary school libraries. User education for adults must be provided through academic, institutional, corporate and public libraries. Given the rate of technological change, this training and assistance will need to be available on an ongoing basis.

#26 -- Massachusetts Board of Library Commissioners

The Environment

SOLINET and its members operate in an environment that is evolving to include new technologies, new information resources, and new information providers. Key factors in this environment include:

- Proliferation of options available to libraries for cataloging, interlibrary loan, and other resource sharing activities.

- Growth of state, local, regional, national and international networks providing infrastructure for cooperative library programming.

- Reallocation of current library resources needed to support new technologies.

- Rapid changes in technology resulting in the need to assess new options, rapid obsolescence, and   increased budgetary demands.

- Growing availability of electronic information, including full-text, from a variety of education, government, and other sources.

- Increasing demand by end-users for improved access to information.

- Ongoing library and archives commitment to cooperation for resource sharing, programming, and implementation of technology.

 # 52 -- SOLINET (Southeastern Library Network Inc.)

Analysis of Strengths, Weaknesses, Opportunities and Threats

CFLC'S Strengths Include:
- A dedicated staff who are committed to the success of the consortium.
- A structure that provides opportunities for libraries in the region to work together.
- The ability to model new programs through research and development efforts.
- A strong program of services such as the Directory of Library Services, CFLC net -- an electronic bulletin board, and the serials union list that enhance an individual library's ability to provide effective service.
- An organizational structure that encourages grass roots participation from all members and values participation in the decision-making process.
- A strong interest in continuing education and training.
- Recognized leadership in statewide networking efforts.
- An action-oriented organization that functions with a minimum of red tape and bureaucracy.
- A commitment to the development of quality products for members.
- Membership and staff which are fully committed to networking and resource sharing.

CFLC'S Weaknesses Include:
- An inability to deliver documents in a timely manner to consortium members.
- A strong reliance on grants for operating costs, research and development costs.
- Limited efforts to communicate the benefit of CFLC membership and services to end users.
- Member libraries that are at vastly different stages of technological development.
- An inability to maintain the OCLC records of selective users, almost half of the member libraries are GAC users.
- Limited staff for implementation of projects.

CFLC'S Opportunities Include:
- The addition of more CFLC members will provide access to more library resources in the region.
- Developments in telecommunications will facilitate distance learning.
- Increased technological capability will permit information to be provided at off-site locations and to user's homes.
- The establishment of alliances with businesses may provide potential for the expansion of CFLC's services.

CFLC'S Threats Include:
- Competition from private information providers.
- Economic conditions that may limit the availability of state and federal funds to support libraries and networks.
- Potential loss of members.

#9 -- Central Florida Library Cooperative

PARADIGM SHIFTS
FOR LIBRARIES AND FOR PALINET

Paradigm shifts are those changes -- positive, negative and neutral -- that will substantially affect the environment in which an organization operates.

During its planning deliberations, the PALINET Board of Trustees identified certain paradigm shifts that will affect libraries and, thus, will affect how libraries use PALINET's services and products. While these shifts probably will not be complete by 1999, the broad outlines of these changes will certainly become clearer in the next few years. Major differences that the Board believes will become apparent during the next four to five years include

- Libraries and information centers increasingly will be viewed as sources of information and less as places or buildings. Concurrently, measures of performance such as library usage will increase in importance, while the number of people visiting libraries in person (turnstile counts) will become less important.

- More information will be available electronically, including the journals of at least one major scholarly publisher. Concurrently, procurement of electronic information resources, or access to them, will consume an increasing portion of library budgets and libraries' needs for cataloging services (e.g., OCLC PRISM Cataloging) to support in-library cataloging will diminish. However, libraries and other information providers will continue to need assistance in organizing both the content of an access to electronic information resources.

- More users will access the library's collection, including electronic resources, from outside the library. Concurrently, libraries will be needed by and will serve users beyond their traditional geographic locality and current constituencies.

- Libraries will have the opportunity to increase their value as information providers to a larger number of users over a broader geographic area through electronic means. Concurrently, the role as depository and guardian of information in printed form will be seen as decreasingly relevant and/or too costly to continue by the average library.

- Libraries will continue to be just one of many information providers available to the public. Concurrently, users will demand more customized information products and delivery methods, and the total expenditure for information services will increase significantly. At the same time, the funding of information services through shared resources (e.g., taxes, tuition) will remain static, while the proportion of information services paid for directly by the individual who accesses and/or uses them will grow.

70

How will these changes affect PALINET?

The PALINET Board and staff, through the strategic planning effort recently concluded, have attempted to position PALINET to be able to

- identify and provide different levels of access to electronic information that suit the varying needs and finances of its members and customers

- facilitate partnerships among and between libraries and other organizations

- act as a clearinghouse of expertise among PALINET members and customers

- deal with the anticipated decrease in demand for OCLC cataloging and ILL services, the primary source of PALINET income today

- expand beyond its traditional membership to include other organizations and individuals with a need for its services and expertise

- develop products and services that will meet new needs and new expectations

- improve its marketing efforts through increased and improved needs assessment

- expand its training, continuing education and consulting roles not only to meet identified needs but to promote new thinking about the present and future of libraries and other information providers.

This updated PALINET Long-Range Strategic Plan reflects an increased emphasis on continual needs assessment, analysis and evaluation. Determining what products and services PALINET needs to be offering through 1999 and beyond is a high priority. Insuring that the products and services PALINET offers are properly developed, priced, managed, evaluated, marketed and publicized is the essential follow-up. Through this plan and its implementation, the Board and staff expect PALINET to remain an essential provider of quality products and services to libraries as they evolve and change.

#43 -- PALINET

Strengths and Weaknesses

The self-study and analysis process identified the following as the Library's greatest strengths:

- Dedicated and well-trained staff;
- Excellent standards of service;
- Strength and quality of collections;
- High level of credibility with governor, legislature, and state agencies;
- High level of credibility with constituent groups throughout the state;
- Strong statutory base for carrying out most service and regulatory responsibilities;
- Well-established formal and informal working relationships with other state agencies, library-related groups, and non-profit agencies.

The Library's greatest weaknesses are identified as:

- Overall lack of adequate resources (staff, materials, equipment, supplies) to meet the needs of all programmatic areas;
- Lack of adequate space for all programmatic and support functions, including reading and research, collection storage and maintenance, and staff workspace;
- Antiquated telephone and electrical systems which are inadequate to meet the demands of the present electronic information and communications environment;
- Poor condition of physical facilities and lack of control over such critical areas as temperature and humidity control, ventilation, and leaking roofs;
- Critical lack of the necessary tools to provide for comprehensive and integrated access to all of the collections;
- Lack of adequate resources to provide critically needed continuing education and staff development;
- Insufficient purchasing power to keep up with the volume and variety of information materials needed;
- Inadequate and unclear statutory authority for the State Archives and Public Records programs;
- Lack of uniform and consistent communication and interactivity with all related state agencies and with constituent groups.

#14 -- Connecticut State Library

THE CONTEXT
Assumptions Concerning The Environment

During the next five years, there will be a growing emphasis on the content of library materials rather than the artifact. Universities and governments will focus on global information as a result of the trend toward the internationalization of information. There will be an increasing recognition that libraries will require larger amounts of information and resources to fill needs beyond the scope of traditional research and teaching.

Program will focus on library cooperation, which will assume greater importance as no library can any longer be self-sufficient.

- Universities will turn more to consortia to solve their problems, and traditional relationships between consortia and their members will be altered by new service models.
- More efforts at local, regional, or subject-related coordinated collection development for moderately-used materials and not just for lesser-used materials will be undertaken, which will require national and international integration into a global resources program.
- Copyright and licensed use questions will not yet be fully resolved, but models will evolve.
- Financial and technological university administrators will assume a greater role in the management of research libraries.
- Continued movement toward focus on "access" as well as "shared ownership" models for library collections will require new agreements and cooperative frameworks.
- The staff resources of CRL and its member libraries will have to be reallocated and retrained to adapt to the demands of the changing environment.

Finance will be a major factor in dictating the pace and scope of the implementation of information technology and the transformation of library cooperation.

- Any slowing in the rate of price increase for library materials will be more than offset by the cost of implementing new technologies.
- Pilot projects will present opportunities for new partnerships and alliances among libraries, private sector providers and users of information, vendors of information technology, and public sector agencies.
- The level for Federal funding of library projects and operations will show little or no significant increase in real terms.
- Competition for private sector grant funding will intensify, and new sources of library funds, such as corporations and non-educational government agencies, will assume a greater role.
- Budgets in state-supported and private universities will not keep pace with cost increases, while Federal support for research will decline.
- As costs rise, universities will face increasing demands for higher quality, accountability and resource-centered management.
- Technology will not necessarily offer less costly means than traditional programming.

73

Technology will continue to transform the manner in which basic library functions are performed.

- Access and delivery will be more automated, with direct user access to information becoming more prevalent.
- More current materials will be published in text encoded electronic formats, and include multimedia links.
- The degree of digitization of existing library collections will depend on advances in cost-effective conversion technology.
- Electronic storage costs will continue to decline in real terms.
- Open systems architectures and much improved search engines will proliferate.

#7 -- Center for Research Libraries

CHAPTER 7

GOALS, OBJECTIVES
&
STRATEGIES

GOALS, OBJECTIVES & STRATEGIES

This chapter is not an effort to rigorously define each component, but rather to provide samples of the content and format used by organizations which submitted their plans. Generally, the goals are broad timeless statements which support the mission and vision with descriptions of what conditions will be pursued. Goals are qualitative statements of the organization's aims. Objectives, strategies, actions and desired results are interpreted in many different ways. Objectives are usually short term measurable statements of achievable results. Actions and strategies are the methods used to achieve the objectives. Strategies are sometimes descriptions of tasks or activities. At other times, strategies are descriptions of the conditions or approaches to using the organization's resources. In some plans, extensive time lines and target dates are documented. Many organizations are focusing on a more strategic approach with only general time frames listed. There seems to be a wide variety of interpretations by library cooperatives for this part of the strategic plan. The style, format, depth and detail in the various plans demonstrate these interpretations.

The organization's goals, objectives and strategies are the "road map" to follow. The benefits of such a plan or map include:
- a clear sense of direction for the organization and active stakeholders,
- documented and agreed upon destination(s) or anticipated accomplishments,
- clearly defined roles and responsibilities,
- a guide for accountability with activity levels tied to allocation of resources.

Everyone can work together more effectively with clearly articulated goals, objectives and strategies. This is one reason that a strategic plan is particularly important for interdependent organizations working in a cooperative environment.

A few of the plans submitted for this publication have a separate page with the goals listed. Most plans only have the goals listed with objectives, strategies or actions detailed under the heading. Most of the examples are reproduced in the integrated format of the plans submitted. Selected examples from different plans are included. The goals, objectives and strategies are not reproduced in total for every plan.

The goals fall into two categories: (1) goals for the organization's infrastructure and operations, (2) goals for services and achievements. This reflects the cooperative and participatory nature of systems. It is interesting to note how responsibility is denoted in different plans. Several charts show the interdependence and specific roles of state agencies, state committees or councils, local and regional cooperatives, as well as, local libraries and members of cooperatives.

Leadership and advocacy are common goals. Cooperatives, systems and networks aim to position libraries as leaders in the forefront of electronic access to information. Multitype library organizations want to influence change and influence libraries to embrace change.

Advocacy goals and activities are related to establishing the role and image of library leadership, community partnerships, information policy and legislative issues.

The emphasis on partnership goals is often with groups outside the library. A multitype cooperative, system or network can act as the partnership agent for groups of member libraries and/or as a catalyst for partnerships with individual libraries. The trend toward community networking/Free-Nets with libraries and multitype library organizations may contribute to the increased emphasis on partnerships. With the many levels of library networking and resource sharing (national, state, regional and local), the partnership and communications goals can be critical to establishing roles for each organization.

Technology goals include the general focus on emerging technology, training and consulting. Internet and the Web have made a dramatic impact on technology goals as libraries seek seamless access and delivery. The Internet has become the key infrastructure for the cooperative organizations and the member libraries. Multitypes are providing Internet for libraries, creating Web pages for libraries and empowering libraries to implement the new technology. Telecommunications policy and technology is a major planning issue. Resource sharing, access to information and delivery are still key goals for multitype library organizations. The efficiency and effectiveness of cooperation is addressed in goals for new services, as well as, core or traditional services. Cooperative purchasing and cooperative access to electronic databases is frequently planned. Internet offers new possibilities for access and delivery. The technology can empower users with more direct access to resources, at the same time libraries are facing challenges of emerging standards, hardware, software and applications.

Continuing education is a very common goal which relates to many of the other goals. The strategies include informal sessions such as user groups, interest group discussions and technology showcases. More formal training and continuing education cover a wide range of topics but often support the new electronic resources. With more electronic resources and more sessions, the need for accessible training centers has emerged. Marketing and communications goals are basic to a collaborative and cooperative organization. The marketing can be outer directed and related to advocacy strategies. The communications and public relations goals can also be directed to the member libraries.

The format of this section of the strategic plan is perhaps as important as the content. Library cooperatives need to be able to easily and continually evaluate their progress against their goals, objectives and strategies. Chapter 8 and Chapter 9 of this book address the evaluation process and format of strategic plans.

1994-1997

CAMLS STRATEGIC PLAN

Goal 1.
Maximize access to resources in and beyond members' collections

Desired Results:
75% of members have Internet Access.
100% of members have holdings on the Union List.
A CAMLS workstation is defined and deployed.

Goal 2.
Develop the financial resources of CAMLS to meet program needs

Desired Results:
CAMLS membership totals 85.
CAMLS financial reserves are increased by $10,000.
CAMLS CE program is positioned to be self-supporting.

Goal 3.
Establish the foundation for an income-generating, cutting-edge Continuing Education program

Desired Results:
Continuing Education is provided in a multi-year sequence of programs organized around member-driven themes.

Goal 4.
Provide expert matchmaking to enhance members' efficiency and effectiveness

Desired Results:
CAMLS facilitates multi-library partnerships and serves as an information clearinghouse in selected areas.

#12 -- Cleveland Area Metropolitan Library System

Goals

1. Continue to offer support for resource sharing activities while pursuing interdependence, seamless access, seamless delivery, and equity of access.

2. Improve individual libraries' ability to offer reference and information services to patrons, including the use of print, electronic and online sources.

3. Work with libraries in the System to enhance their ability to implement technology and electronic resources in their operations.

4. Offer quality continuing education opportunities for diverse needs and audiences, especially within primary and secondary System service roles.

5. Offer consultation services within the primary and secondary System service roles; facilitate consultation among peers.

6. Work with library development leaders for reciprocal support, feedback, and cooperation.

7. Use resources as available for special projects, such as the cooperative video license.

Goal 1
Continue to offer support for resource sharing activities while pursuing interdependence, seamless access, seamless delivery, and equity of access.

- Shift 70% of sites currently dependent on ILL resource center service toward more independent ILL. (June 1997)
- Maintain existing resource center contracts during development and transition toward new goals.
- Work towards a broader means of electronic access to Nebraska libraries' holdings, either through a union catalog or through other innovative methods. (August 1995)
- Examine and choose the most efficient and cost effective delivery system for interlibrary loan in southeast Nebraska. (August 1995)
- Develop educational requirements for the use of the system resource centers. (July 1995)
- Incorporate policies of responsibility in conjunction with use of the ILL/Reference services; include Rule Statements and guidelines divided by the system and enforced by the Center. (July 1995)
- Create an ILL training video for System members' use. (July 1996)
- Continue to analyze and implement charges for use of System resource centers.
- Announce the fade of the 800# for resource centers; discontinue 800#s. (August 96/December 96)

Goal 2

Improve individual libraries' ability to offer reference and information services to patrons, including the use of print, electronic and online sources.

- Work with the Nebraska Library Commission to offer subsidized access to databases such as OCLC's FirstSearch. (December 1995)
- Offer Internet training and access assistance. (ongoing)
- Offer reference materials training, using the STAR Reference Manual (Fall 1995/Spring 1996/Fall 1997)
- Offer reference interview training in conjunction with STAR Manual workshops. (Fall 1995/Spring 1996/Fall 1997)

Goal 3

Work with libraries in the System to enhance their ability to implement technology and electronic resources in their operations.

- Offer technology showcase workshop which highlights emerging technologies. (Fall 1995)
- Assist libraries in obtaining financial assistance for hardware purchases. (ongoing)
- Work with the Nebraska Library Commission and *Nebrask@ Interactive* to provide uniform and affordable Internet access. (January 1996)
- Assist libraries in developing Internet connections, including SLIP/PPP connections. (ongoing)
- Continue to provide a site license for Alliance Plus (the Follett bibliographic CD for data conversion). (ongoing)
- Employ a part time technology consultant to make onsite visits to libraries who have questions and concerns in technology development and implementation. (July 1995)

Goal 4

Offer quality continuing education opportunities for diverse needs and audiences, especially within primary and secondary System service roles.

- In addition to continuing education opportunities highlighted in previous goal statements, offer training in multi-cultural programming, children's and young adult programming, community analysis, people skills, trustee training, and basic library skills. (ongoing)
- Facilitate interest group discussions and meetings, such as the Follett user group meetings. (ongoing)
- Continue to poll membership for continuing education needs. (ongoing)
- Work with other regional library systems to deliver continuing education programs. (ongoing)

Goal 5
Offer consultation services within the primary and secondary System service roles; facilitate consultation among peers.

- Provide WATS line to the System office for member use.
- Publish a newsletter 10 times per year, to include information on library development.
- Provide incentives for mentoring among librarians, including grants to participants. (August 1996)
- Continue to provide support for Children's Service through the provision of a Juvenile Resource Center.
- Review current Children's Services; make appropriate recommendations. (April 1996)
- Continue to provide professional journals for routing to member libraries. Increase or change titles as needed for emerging interests. (ongoing)
- Purchase a System car for Administrator travel. (July 1995)

Goal 6
Work with library development leaders for reciprocal support, feedback, and cooperation.

- System Administrator will attend meetings with peers and with Nebraska Library Commission staff. (ongoing)
- System Administrator will participate in broad planning initiatives in Nebraska, keeping Southeast Library System goals and objectives in the forefront of discussions. (ongoing)

Goal 7
Use resources as available for special projects, such as the cooperative video license.

- Provide subsidies for the purchase of public performance rights for the airing of video productions in member libraries. (January 1996 and January 1997)
- Investigate the potential for author visits to System libraries; help facilitate visits. (ongoing)
- Create a System Handbook of services and members. (August 1995) Make this Handbook available in electronic format. (July 1996)

TIMELINE:

July 1995
Employ a part time technology consultant
Implement educational requirements for the use of the resource centers
Incorporate policies of responsibility for resource center use.
Purchase a System car for Administrator travel.
August 1995
Union Catalog of Holdings
Choose most effective delivery system for ILL
Southeast Library System Handbook
Fall 1995
Reference training
Technology showcase
December 1995
Subsidized access to online databases available
January 1996
Internet access for libraries
Spring 1996
Reference training
April 1996
Children's Services program recommendations
July 1996
ILL/Reference training video
SELS Handbook: Electronic version
August 1996
Announce fade out of 800# for ILL/Reference
Mentoring incentives
December 1996
Discontinue ILL/Ref 800#
June 1997
70% of resource center dependent users shifted to direct ILL
Fall 1997
Reference training

Ongoing Activities:
Internet, etc. training
Variety of workshops
Consultation activities
Newsletters
Technology purchase assistance to libraries
WATS to office
Resource centers
Video license
SLIP/PPP connections for libraries
Alliance Plus provision

#51 -- Southeast Nebraska Library System

GOALS

Governance and Organization
Promote SEFLIN as a membership organization that supports and encourages resource sharing and joint use of technology among libraries in the Southeast Florida community.

Advocacy and Leadership
Establish SEFLIN as an advocate for libraries in Southeast Florida by forming alliances and partnerships with other organizations.

Emerging Technologies
Assist member libraries to identify and use strategic and emerging technologies and promote joint use of technology.

Information Resources
Support the continuing needs of members to cooperatively collect, organize, preserve and disseminate information resources for Southeast Florida residents.

SEFLIN Free-Net
Continue SEFLIN's role in providing local, government and community information to Southeast Florida residents.

Continuing Education and Training
Provide and coordinate opportunities for continuing education to increase a library staff member's ability to serve library users.

#50 b. Southeast Florida Library Information Network, Inc.

Goal 2:

ADVOCACY AND LEADERSHIP
Establish SEFLIN as an advocate for libraries in Southeast Florida by forming alliances and partnerships with other organizations.

Objectives

2.1 Develop marketing and public relations activities to promote SEFLIN libraries' contribution to the economic and social well-being of Southeast Florida.

2.2 Use SEFLIN's local successes as a way to increase local, state, regional and national recognition and attract funds and awards.

2.3 Establish an advocacy network comprised of the Free-Net Advisory Committee, library friends and trustees to promote the importance of libraries, resource sharing and the role of libraries in the information age.

Strategies

- a. Continue the publication and wide-distribution of the SEFLIN newsletter in print and electronic format. (Ongoing)

- b. Form partnerships with groups that allow SEFLIN to increase its contact with community, government and business decision-makers. (Ongoing)

- c. Write and place press releases and articles about SEFLIN activities, services, and pilot projects in the local, state, regional, and national library press. (Ongoing)

- d. Participate actively in meetings with the Florida Library Network Council, SOLINET's Network Council, other library cooperatives, ASCLA and other related groups. (Ongoing)

- e. Develop targeted communication tools that can be used to represent SEFLIN to potential partners and member institutions. (1996 and ongoing)

- f. Establish ad hoc groups of marketing and community relations librarians to plan specific activities for promoting SEFLIN in the media and with other libraries. (1997/98)

- g. Expand communication about SEFLIN in member libraries so more staff, on all levels, are familiar with SEFLIN's programs and services. (1997/98)

- h. Work with the member libraries and the Florida Library Association to sponsor SEFLIN activities to assist with local, regional, statewide and national efforts to increase funding and support for libraries and networks. (1997/98)

GOAL 3:

EMERGING TECHNOLOGIES
Assist member libraries to identify and use strategic and emerging technologies and promote joint use of technology.

Objectives
> 3.1 Assume a leadership role in identifying emerging technologies responsive to member needs and services.

> 3.2 Develop pilot projects to experiment with joint use of technologies.

Strategies
- a. Sponsor an emerging technologies session at SEFLIN's annual meeting and other sessions throughout the year. (Ongoing)

- b. Establish an ongoing forum that assists members in planning cooperatively for the use of new technologies. (Ongoing)

- c. Investigate the digitization of library resources. (Ongoing)

- d. Provide information about "hot" issues under discussion by the Florida Library Network Council, the Distance Learning Network, and other state, regional, and national groups to SEFLIN members. (Ongoing)

- e. Encourage library staff to participate in existing listservs on emerging technologies and explore the feasibility of developing a SEFLIN listserv on emerging technologies. (1996/97)

- f. Publish a bulletin with tips about using existing technology and information about emerging technologies. (1997/98)

- g. Provide funding for members and staff to attend conferences on emerging technologies and develop a method for reporting information back to SEFLIN members and electronically archiving information. (1997/98)

- h. Explore new technologies for electronic document delivery and expand service to additional SEFLIN libraries. (1997/98)

- i. Focus on electronic security issues needed to protect access to electronic information. (1997/98)

- j. Investigate options for direct delivery of materials to users via commercial document delivery options. (1998/99)

- k. Use distance learning technology for delivering continuing education and facilitating committee activities. (1998/99)

GOAL 4:

INFORMATION RESOURCES
Support the continuing needs of members to cooperatively collect, organize, preserve and disseminate information resources for Southeast Florida residents.

Objectives
4.1 Identify areas in which SEFLIN members can work together to develop and/or broker services on behalf of member libraries.

4.2 Enhance the resource sharing and document delivery capabilities of member libraries.

4.3 Expand traditional library services to more user-friendly, electronic, remotely accessible services.

Strategies

- a. Explore the cooperative purchase of electronic information resources. (1996/97)

- b. Assist member libraries in efforts to preserve materials and collections. (1996/97)

- c. Work cooperatively to assist government documents librarians to deliver electronic government information. (1997/98)

- d. Seek opportunities for member libraries to participate in cooperative collection development. (1996/97)

- e. Foster cooperative cataloging services and bibliographic maintenance. (1997/98)

- f. Use the collective purchasing power of SEFLIN's members to secure the maximum vendor discount for information products, library equipment, technology, and telecommunications. (1997/98)

- g. Identify unique library collections appropriate for digitization in efforts to expand access to these resources. (1997/98)

- h. Evaluate the SEFLIN courier service and explore other options for providing delivery. (1997/98)

- i. Maintain, enhance and evaluate the SEFLIN library card program. (Ongoing)

- j. Explore options for expanding electronic document delivery. (1996/97)

- k. Investigate methods for streamlining the interlibrary loan process by allowing greater end-user participation. (1997/98)

GOAL 5:

SEFLIN Free-Net
Continue SEFLIN's role in providing local, government and community information to Southeast Florida residents.

Objectives
>   5.1 Continue and enhance the SEFLIN Free-Net as a regional resource.
>
>   5.2 Implement technological improvements to facilitate user access to the Free-Net and on-line information.

Strategies
- a. Develop a plan for a graphical user interface (GUI) and manage the migration of existing Free-Net content to a web-server. (1996/97)

- b. Maintain the operation of three county editions of the SEFLIN Free-Net. (Ongoing)

- c. Expand, enhance, and stabilize the operations of the SEFLIN Free-Net, its advisory Committee and sub-committee structure. (1997/98)

- d. Continue the recruitment, training and support for Information Providers and increase the number of Information Providers. (Ongoing)

- e. Continue training sessions for member libraries and the community and enhance the development of the volunteer corps. (Ongoing)

- f. Continue marketing the SEFLIN Free-Net with a focus on its goals and accomplishments. (Ongoing)

- g. Cooperate with other institutions and community groups on joint projects that support the overall philosophy of the Free-Net and public access to information. (Ongoing)

- h. Support the efforts of the education community to share information regionally and provide information through the Free-Net. (Ongoing)

- i. Promote the use of the Free-Net as a reference tool by member libraries. (1997/98)

- j. Develop a plan for financial stability and fund raising. (1997/98)

- k. Develop a plan to examine and clarify the role of academic libraries in the Free-Net. (1997/98)

- l. Work cooperatively with other free-Nets and community networks in the state and nation to share information and assist in the development of other Free-Nets. (Ongoing)

>   *#50 a. -- Southeast Florida Library Information Network, Inc.*

Plan of Service

I. Reference and Technology

1. Strengthen reference resources available to Bergen County residents
   A. Hire a consultant to develop recommendations for enhancing reference service to the public
   B. Encourage continued cooperation between member libraries in providing reference services

2. Increase flexibility of DRA workstations with continued implementation of PC based, rather than dumb terminal, software

3. Improve the user friendliness of the OPAC interface
   A. Request focus groups to work with BCCLS staff members on PC and non-PC products

4. Work toward preferential telecommunications rates for libraries and patrons communicating with libraries
   A. Request discounts from the telecommunications industry
   B. Request support from public officials, if necessary

5. Develop the role of the Internet as a major vehicle for library service
   A. Investigate school resources for local Internet developments
   B. Address non-bibliographic files, such as community information files

6. Implement CD-ROM as part of the BCCLS profile
   A. Catalog CD-ROM circulating and reference items
   B. Enhance resources for CD-ROM use in the library

II. Communication, Cooperation and In-Service Training

1. Establish a staff development committee with a two-year charge to determine the viability of said committee to:
   A. Continue staff exchanges for various departments on a regular basis
   B. Arrange professional development programs focusing on topics of interest
   C. Provide guidelines for writing manuals covering basic library operations
   D. Encourage visits to libraries beyond Bergen County for examples of effective service and programs
   E. Sponsor one or two Publisher's Days each year: CD-ROM, children, reference, vocational guidance, etc.

2. Continue system-wide small group meetings at least twice a year

3. Continue training sessions on technology and required skills at the BCCLS office and on site, as appropriate

4. Improve availability of resources in all formats
   A. Investigate and encourage cooperative collection development
   B. Negotiate vendor discounts

III. Alternate Funding

1. Provide continued support for BCCLS services with fees from contracting libraries and school districts

2. Use grants as the major source of funding to initiate new services when possible

3. Encourage partnerships with private and public entities where appropriate

4. Approach Bergen County towns without libraries to sign direct contracts with BCCLS

IV. Public Awareness

1. Keep library news in the media

2. Continue programs for the public regarding new technologies in our libraries

3. Become involved with technology related groups, such as the New Jersey Cable TV Association, SeniorNet, and computer clubs

4. Coordinate a county-wide book related event (possibly every two years)

#2 -- Bergen County Cooperative Library System

C. Role Identification and Detail of MOLO's Strategic Plan 1996-1999

1. Continuing Education

Role: *Offer continuing education opportunities for professional, staff, and trustees to improve and enhance library services and operations.*

- Produce an Annual Continuing Education Calendar
- Offer recurring basic courses in library education (orientations, reference, children's, etc.)
- Develop issues forums for trustees and library administrators
- Identify and develop program tracks for programmatic skills building (Reference 101, 201, etc.)
- Introduce a learning component into every meeting.

2. Technology Support

Role: *Provide ongoing support and awareness for MOLO members to adopt and manage new technologies into their libraries.*

- Hire a MOLO Technologist specializing in on-site teaching and consultation
- Complete a technology training center at the MOLO Office
- Develop a first point of contact helpdesk for PC's, OPLIN, and the Internet
- Provide consultation services for automating libraries
- Provide on-site support for PC troubleshooting
- Provide on-site Internet training for member library staffs and trustees.

3. Interlibrary Lending and Resource Sharing

Role: *Facilitate a means of guaranteeing that library users can get information and materials not found in their libraries.*

- Develop an automated interlibrary loan system which can accommodate all member libraries regardless of automated circulation system
- Further develop the article photocopying service with greater access and faster turnaround time on delivery at less expense than mediate services
- Provide reference backup systems for library members unable to answer patron questions from their own resources
- Develop reciprocal borrowing arrangements among libraries.

4. Information production

Role: *Coordinate production of information which help libraries analyze current issues and provide services to their users.*

91

- Create a regularly updated Union List of Periodicals in print and non-print formats
- Publish an expanded monthly MOLO MEMO newsletter
- Be able to provide camera-ready desktop publishing (reproducible on copy machines) for members libraries
- Publish and distribute Summer Reading Club supplement and other resource manuals of value to member libraries
- Create, publish and distribute reference tools (union lists, inventories on special collections, etc.)
- Investigate publishing/maintenance of local information on the Internet
- Develop "Web pages" or public access points for all member libraries available through the Internet in conjunction with other statewide initiatives (e.g. OPLIN, OhioLINK, INFOhio, etc.)

#31 -- MOLO Regional Library System

LEADERSHIP

Strategies 2001: By the year 2001. . .libraries anticipate trends in their own service communities, society as a whole, and an evolving technological environment. They provide leadership in the midst of change.

SWRLSS Long Range Plan: Define, communicate, and promote the role of systems, libraries and librarians.

Strategies 2001 Strategies		SWRLSS Long Range Plan Objectives
1. Each library entity develops and implements a plan for its own growth and development.	L1	Assist local libraries with planning Maintain SWRLSS Long Range Plan
2. Appropriate statewide groups develop and disseminate guidelines, standards, plans and laws to provide guidance in planning.	L2	Actively participate in regional, statewide and national committees and library organizations.
3. The Colorado library community regularly assesses and reviews state-funded services provided to libraries which help them service their constituencies.	L3	Assess, review, and implement state-funded, or state funding, programs. Engage in cooperative projects with other systems.
4. Librarians and their governing authorities and/or advisory bodies are leaders within their own constituencies, actively advocating library services and information access.	L4	Inform and educate librarians and other decision-makers Advocate for library service and information access.
5. Decision makers at all levels provide sufficient resources to attain quality library services for all Colorado citizens.	L5	Seek and help members seek adequate funding to respond to system members' needs.
6. Library entities forge partnerships to expand and enhance libraries and library services.	L6	Advocate and forge public/private and inter-library partnerships.
	L7	Connect member libraries with each other, SWRLSS, and outside entities.

SERVICES

Strategies 2001: By the year 2001 every person in Colorado receives library materials and answers quickly, provided by welcoming, knowledgeable staff through user-friendly technology and relevant library collections and resources. Libraries contribute to people's lives as informed and productive citizens; help them solve problems, stimulate their imaginations, enrich their lives. They support individual growth, recreational interests, and professional, economic, and cultural development.

SWRLSS Long Range Plan: Enhance and improve the services offered by member libraries.

Strategies 2001		SWRLSS Long Range Plan Objectives
1. Libraries develop collections, programs, and services to meet the diverse needs of their individual constituencies.	S1	Identify and meet diverse needs of system members.
3. Library staffs continuously update their professional skills in order to provide the highest level of service to their constituencies.	S3	Provide members with the opportunity to update their professional skills Provide assistance with problem solving. Update system staff skills.
4. Library entities enable users to find, evaluate, and use information to their best advantage and as independently as possible, in accordance with their individual missions.	S4	Assist system members with standards and guidelines.
5. School districts adopt and implement the principles of information literacy, ensuring students access to both professional staff and current resources.	S5	
	S6	Assist system members with implementing technology.
	S7	Provide for economies of scale.

RESOURCE SHARING

Strategies 2001: By the year 2001 every person in Colorado has equal and consistent access to information through a seamless web of libraries which participate in a global network of libraries and information providers. People use a variety of access points and types of libraries without restriction. They depend on library access, services and staff, whose costs are both clear and defensible. The word "library" is synonymous with information access, whether one travels there physically or electronically.

SWRLSS Long Range Plan: Facilitate member libraries' awareness of, and access to, information in all formats.

Strategies 2001		SWRLSS Long Range Plan
1. Libraries are vital links to resources on the global information network.	RS1	Assist system members with access to, and use of, the global information network (internet).
2. ACLIN provides an easily used, vital source of information about and access to library, community and government resources	RS2	Advocate continued participation in and development of ACLIN.
3. Libraries and library users request and receive information and materials by the most effective and cost-efficient methods.	RS3	Coordinate and improve interlibrary loan, courier, and reference referral services for the region. Promote walk-in and electronic access to library resources.

The following table repeats the NEEDS of system members, and relates to the numbers above (L3, S4, etc.) that indicate ways in which SWRLSS is attempting to meet these needs.

Technology
- Training — S1 & S2
- Hardware and software selection — S6
- Internet use — R5
- Telecommunications consultation — S6 & RS1
- Automated systems — S6
- Getting records into ACLIN — RS2
- Ethical considerations of internet use — S6
- Troubleshooting and diagnosis — S6
- Networking (LANs and WANs) — S6

Basic Skills Training
- Reference — S3
- Programming — S3
- Management — S3
- Marketing — S3
- Collection Development — S3
- Technical Services — S3
- Interlibrary Loan — S3
- Planning — S3 & L1

Standards implementation
- School — S4 & S5
- Public — S4 & S5

Funding
- Grant writing — S3
- Cooperative grants — L6

#54 -- Southwest Regional Library Service System

95

THE STRATEGIC PLAN

GOAL I   **Coordinate technological development, training and support for Network members in the Region.**

OBJECTIVES

A.   <u>Develop Standards and Protocols for the use of Technology in Member Libraries.</u>
   1. Based on requirements implicit in Regional programs, identify minimum configuration and standards for equipment, software and services, and incorporate these into recommendations to member libraries, beginning in the third quarter of 1995.
   2. Work with the State Librarian to assure the application of appropriate standards and protocols to any program of statewide interconnectivity.
   3. Work with other library groups -- such as professional associations, consortia, library schools -- to coordinate technology-centered activities.

B.   <u>Establish and Support a Program of Technological Training for Member Libraries.</u>
   1. Investigate member training need during the first quarter of 1995.
   2. Establish a variety of training programs for libraries on using technology, starting with basic computer/modem skills, during the third quarter of 1995.

C.   <u>Establish and Sustain a Program of Technological Assistance to Member Libraries.</u>
   1. Develop a job description for a technology consultant, and based upon the parameters contained in the description, hire or contract with a technology consultant in the first quarter of 1995.
   2. Explore the appropriate way for persons in the Region to share their technological expertise with member libraries in the second quarter of 1995.
   3. Explore the parameters for establishing a Regional hot line number for technological assistance in the third quarter of 1995.
   4. Establish the Cooperative as the organizer and identifier of group purchasing arrangements for members in the first quarter of 1996.

GOAL II   **Promote, develop and support electronic access to information resources and on-line linkages for and among Region members.**

OBJECTIVES

A.   <u>Assure Access to a Freenet for Region Members.</u>
   1. Identify the necessary requirements for providing access to a freenet by the second quarter of 1995.
   2. Conduct a workshop for participating libraries on features of and hardware requirements for using a freenet during the third quarter of 1995.
   3. Establish access to the freenet by the second quarter of 1996.
   4. Conduct hands-on training workshops, preferably on-site, for each participating library by the fourth quarter of 1996.
   5. Develop an evaluation by the fourth quarter of 1996.

B. Support a Program to Provide Full Internet Access for Member Libraries.
1. Explore the feasibility of establishing Internet access for member libraries in the second quarter of 1995.
2. Based upon the feasibility study, establish a method for member libraries to acquire access to full Internet services in the fourth quarter of 1995.

C. Establish the Basis for Cooperative Access to Electronic Resources.
1. Ensure that all members have access to e-mail by the fourth quarter of 1996.
2. Investigate alternative methods, including but not necessarily limited to the establishment of electronic reference centers, that would enable all members to have electronic access to reference resources in the second quarter of 1995.
3. Investigate Group Access to OCLC and comparable methodologies of interlibrary resource sharing for all members in the second quarter of 1996.
4. Investigate the Cooperative's potential for coordinating or facilitating a Regional program of commercially-based document delivery in the third quarter of 1996.
5. Implement the methodologies recommended under II.C.2, II.C.3, and II.C.4 by the second quarter of 1997.

D. Support the Development of Unique Regional Data Bases.
1. Identify appropriate sources, such as newspapers or other local community information resources, for the creation of unique Regional data bases in the third quarter of 1997.
2. Begin to create or achieve access to these databases for all members by the fourth quarter of 1997.

GOAL III   **Provide advocacy and leadership for technology on behalf of Region members.**

OBJECTIVES

A. Develop an Advocacy Program based on Technology Needs Targeting Policy-makers and Funding Bodies.
1. Assist member libraries to assess current levels of technology and project future needs in the first quarter of 1995.
2. Assist member libraries to prioritize their needs and develop a recommended implementation schedule by the second quarter of 1995.
3. Develop an on-going program of information dissemination, using the consistent theme of libraries as both providers of and gateways to information as the basis for an advocacy program in the third quarter of 1995.

B. Identify and Tap Sources of Funding to Implement Technology within the Region.
1. Seek grants and other funding on behalf of the Region and, as appropriate, member libraries beginning in the first quarter of 1995.
2. Establish the Cooperative as a clearing house for grant information by forming a standing committee to monitor the availability of implementation grants for technology in the fourth quarter of 1995.

C. Expand the Scope of Influence for Libraries through the Development of Information Partnerships.
1. Establish a working group of representatives from nonlibrary information organizations in the first quarter of 1995.
2. Establish the basis for nonlibrary organizations to support the freenet in the second quarter of 1995.

GOAL IV   **Position libraries as being in the forefront of electronic access to information.**

OBJECTIVES

A. Promote the Value of Libraries as Information Providers and Mediators.
1. Empower a public relations committee to work with Regional staff to develop a technology-related theme that would consistently permeate all Regional publications, announcements and displays in the second quarter of 1995.
2. Develop a method of advertising access to the freenet in the third quarter of 1995.
3. Plan for an interactive library channel utilizing an appropriate carrier in the region in the second quarter of 1997.

B. Promote the Concept of Universal Access to Resources.
1. Organize a Regional task force to create an advertising campaign on how libraries promote universal access to resources in the first quarter of 1996.
2. Begin to publicize how technology makes it possible to get information by coordinating library- and nonlibrary-based resources in the second quarter of 1996.

GOAL V   **Ensure the continuing excellence and quality of technology programs and services within the Cooperative.**

OBJECTIVES

A. Establish and Maintain Appropriate Evaluative Techniques and Mechanisms for Components of the Plan.
1. Appoint a task force to prepare an evaluative methodology in the third quarter of 1995.
2. Present a draft of the proposed evaluation program for Board review in the fourth quarter of 1995.

B. Undertake an On-going Evaluation and Review of this Plan.
1. Establish a methodology for annual evaluation and review in the third quarter of 1995.
2. Conduct the first evaluation and present a progress report in the second quarter of 1996.
3. Annually review the plan to ensure quality, incorporating the results of program evaluations.

#10 a. -- Central Jersey Regional Library Cooperative

General Goals

CMLE seeks to:

A. Improve library/media/information services in the CMLE area through cooperative efforts;

B. Develop and facilitate cooperative library/media/information activities in the CMLE area;

C. Provide assistance and coordination for participating library and media agencies in carrying out desired cooperation;

D. Work through the Council of Cooperating Libraries and with the Minnesota Department of Children, Families and Learning, including the Office of Library Development and Services, and other agencies and Minnesota library and media associations for the improvement and extension of library services in the state.

Communications/Continuing Education

A. Goals

CMLE seeks to:

1. Improve communication among library/media/information agencies in its area;
2. Keep members, potential members, and other interested personnel informed of cooperative developments in the library/media/information field;
3. Serve as a means of increased participation in the development of mutually satisfactory cooperative library/media/information activities in the CMLE area;
4. Share CMLE experiences in multitype library cooperation with the other multitype library cooperation systems in the state.
5. Explore and implement new technology to promote improved communications among member libraries/media centers.

B. Objectives

1. Various means of communication will be used.
2. Efforts will be made to assess the effectiveness of communication used.
3. Work will be done to improve the targeting and effectiveness of communication.
4. Alternative communication means will be considered.
5. CMLE activities will be reported to the Office of Library Development and Services.

C. Tasks

Target Dates:

1. The Governing Board should:

   a. Provide for the development and management of a communications system; **CONTINUOUS**

   b. Consider and determine, upon recommendations of the Advisory Committee, changes to be made in the communications system; **CONTINUOUS**

2. CMLE staff will:

   a Create a CMLE home page on the Internet; **Fall 1997**

   b. Issue the newsletter on a periodic basis; **CONTINUOUS**

   c. Update the mailing list to include changes in, and additions to, personnel; **CONTINUOUS**

d. Seek feedback on the effectiveness of the newsletter through an annual survey and interaction with participants; **CONTINUOUS**

e. Together with the Advisory Committee, make recommendations to the Governing Board on the nature and continuance of the newsletter; **CONTINUOUS**

f. Seek user experience with the directory through periodic survey and interaction with member libraries/media centers; **FALL 1996**

g. Maintain up-to-date directory information as a computer-based file; **CONTINUOUS**

h. Produce electronic directory listing including Internet addresses and make this information available through a CMLE home page on the Internet; **FALL 1997**

i. Distribute agendas, minutes, and reports of activities to Advisory Committee, Governing Board and Office of Library Development and Services; **AS APPROPRIATE**

j. Provide CMLE Director's Internet address to all CMLE members; **CONTINUOUS**

3. The Governing Board should budget for appropriate telecommunications in order to provide equitable access for all CMLE members to CMLEÕs services through such things as incoming "800" numbers for both CMLE's telephone and fax service; **FALL 1996**

4. CMLE staff will:

a. Respond to queries about CMLE; **CONTINUOUS**

b. Consider and plan for future telecommunications use; **1996-2001**

5. The Governing Board should budget for continuing education workshops including, but not limited to, current and future information access through telecommunications; **1996-2001**

6. The CMLE staff and Continuing Education subcommittee will:

a. Seek to co-sponsor and advertise workshops held in the area for the benefit of the library/media/information community; **CONTINUOUS**

b. Identify needed areas of workshops through surveys and network interaction; **CONTINUOUS**

c. Plan for workshops to be held in various locations; **ANNUALLY**

d. Plan for a program to be held in conjunction with the annual meeting; **SUMMER 1996-2001**

e. Assess previous workshops; **SUMMER 1996-2001**

f. Work with Advisory Committee in recommending needed workshops for funding to Governing Board; **SPRING 1996-2001**

7. CMLE staff will plan and organize an informational meeting for area legislators; **FALL 1996**

8. The Advisory Committee will evaluate and make recommendations for future legislative information meetings; **1996-2001**

9. The Governing Board should provide for annual meetings; **1996-2001**

10. The CMLE staff will:

a. In conjunction with library/media/information associations, set a date for the annual meeting; **ANNUALLY**

b. Make initial arrangements for meeting time and place; **JUNE/JULY 1996**

    c. Work with other associations in setting program; **SUMMER 1996**

    d. Publicize annual meeting; **SEPT. - OCT. 1996**

    e. Make final arrangements; **SEPT. - OCT. 1996**

    f. Coordinate annual meeting; **SEPT. - OCT. 1996**

11. The Governing Board and Advisory Committee will consider the nature of future annual meetings; **WINTER 1996-1997**

12. The CMLE will seek the continued cooperation of affiliated associations for its annual meetings; **1996-2001**

13. CMLE staff will be available to meet with library/media/information groups and others of related interest; **CONTINUOUS**

14. The responsibility for telecommunications development will be shared between the Advisory Committee and the CMLE staff; **AS NEEDED**

15. CMLE staff and Advisory Committee will study the need for a regional plan for the preservation of library and media materials; **WINTER 1996-1997**

16. Upon the request of CMLE member libraries/media centers, CMLE staff should attend (when feasible) board meetings of CMLE members to promote multitype cooperation; **AS REQUESTED**

#11 -- Central Minnesota Libraries Exchange

GOALS

Goals are timeless, unbounded statements that describe the conditions or attributes to be attained: what the world will be like as a result, at least in part, of what the organization will do.

The Board of Trustees believes the resources and actions of PALINET should be applied to achieve the following five goals:

1. **SERVICES AND PRODUCTS**
   PALINET will be a leader in providing services and products responsive to the evolving needs of libraries and information centers.

   Comment: This goal emphasizes, among other things, the need to maintain and strengthen the range of services and related support and to enhance the corporation's technological capabilities for the benefit of members and their clientele.

2. **OCLC SERVICE**
   PALINET will provide member libraries expert and timely advice, training and support in the effective use of OCLC products and services.

   Comment: This goal recognizes the need to devote sufficient staff and resources to provide quality OCLC support.

3. **ADVOCACY**
   PALINET will be an effective voice for librarians in shaping the development and use of information technology.

   Comment: This goal emphasizes PALINET's role on behalf of its members and other libraries in helping to shape the development and use of information technology for the benefit of its members and their clientele.

4. **PARTNERING**
   PALINET will enhance member service through partnerships and alliances.

   Comment: Successful enterprises achieve results through effective partnerships and alliances, and PALINET sees this as an important goal for the future both of its members and of the corporation itself.

5. **INFLUENCE CHANGE**
   PALINET will influence libraries to embrace technological change.

   Comment: This goal addresses the inevitable changes that libraries will undergo with increasing rapidity during the next several years, and implies that PALINET will work with its members to adopt and apply beneficial technologies for improved service to members and their clientele.

CONDITIONS AND STRATEGIES

Conditions describe why a goal is important. They describe the nature of the current or anticipated environment that the organization will seek to change.

Strategies are ways in which the organization will focus its resources and actions to achieve the objective.

In the following pages, each goal is restated and the conditions and strategies related to the goal are presented.

GOAL. 1   **SERVICES AND PRODUCTS**
PALINET will be a leader in providing services and products responsive to the evolving needs of libraries and information centers.

Conditions
This goal addresses:

The need --
- For flexibility in marketing
- To delineate PALINET's role in an increasingly confusing and changing information environment
- Of libraries to have an organization that evaluates products and provides the best value for their dollar
- Of libraries to avoid impediments of local procedures

The opportunity --
- For product development
- To achieve a leadership role in targeted product and service areas
- For members to take advantage of cutting-edge technology through PALINET
- To winnow choices and direct libraries toward the most cost-effective and productive options
- To expand market share beyond members

Strategies

1. Target critical areas in which to develop and/or broker products and/or services where PALINET can be a leader, maximize use of resources, and leverage the investment.
2. Establish and maintain an evaluation process for the products and services offered.
3. Maintain a high level of customer/member communication and service.
4. Establish a marketing plan for products and services.
5. Conduct needs assessment and market analysis for continuing education.
6. Provide comprehensive, integrated solutions.

GOAL 2.   <u>OCLC SERVICE</u>

PALINET will provide member libraries expert and timely advice, training and support in the effective use of OCLC products and services.

Conditions

This goal addresses:

The need --
- Of members to link with OCLC
- For ongoing training and support for libraries in a critical aspect of their operations and services

The opportunity to --
- Bring value to membership and maintain OCLC as a central element of PALINET's operations
- Market and sell the products and services of, and maintain a special relationship with the leader in information technology (OCLC) that member libraries could not develop independently
- Provide other products and services to libraries that result from a stable financial base provided by core services and products

Strategies

1. Increase expertise of PALINET staff in the application and use of OCLC product and services.
2. Increase use of OCLC products and services.
3. Develop new methods of delivering support and training for OCLC (e.g., regional offices, distance learning, on-site training, self-paced training).
4. Determine who uses OCLC services and employ this knowledge in product evaluation and support.
5. Design training for a changing "worker group."
6. Conduct ongoing evaluation of OCLC services, training, and support, and address areas of weakness.

GOAL 3.   <u>ADVOCACY</u>

PALINET will be an effective voice for librarians in shaping the development and use of information technology.

Conditions

This goal addresses:

The need --
- To influence the nature of services available to PALINET customers
- To influence change so that libraries can continue and grow as viable organizations
- For libraries to represent their constituents' needs for information when and where they need it

The opportunity to --
- Participate in regional and national forums where policies affecting library and information services are being discussed and promulgated
- Learn more about the problems faced by libraries and information centers and the issues that are of importance to them
- Work with providers of products and services needed by members and customers so that these products and services do indeed represent cost-effective solutions to member needs

Strategies

1. Participate in the development of policies that affect the future of libraries and information services (e.g., National Information Infrastructure, telecommunication, American Library Association, state libraries, American Society for Information Science).
2. Engage in increased dialogue with members to identify problems and critical issues for them. Increase awareness of these problems and issues through such approaches as working with teams from individual libraries, interaction with focus groups and onsite visits.
3. Increase influence on providers to develop products and services responsive to member needs (e.g. OCLC, SilverPlatter, Bell Atlantic, document delivery services).

GOAL 4.   **PARTNERING**

PALINET will enhance member services through partnerships and alliances.

Conditions

This goal addresses:

The need --
- To better serve members
- For "pooled" resources
- To operate more efficiently
- For libraries to establish links into electronic networks and use them effectively

The opportunity to --
- Enhance the image of PALINET as a prime provider
- Access greater expertise
- Expand products and services of PALINET
- Develop services/products that serve a larger member/customer base
- Reduce the risk inherent in new product development
- Increase PALINET visibility both within and outside traditional markets
- Do more with fewer staff
- Focus on one or more new development areas
- Facilitate the "discovery" process
- Reduce costs for libraries (e.g., discounts, increased productivity)
- Influence change through partners

Strategies

1. Identify, implement and maintain effective partnerships to achieve PALINET's goals and objectives.
2. Reassess existing partnerships and determine what changes are needed (modify, expand, end).
3. Foster formation of beneficial partnerships between members and among other organizations.
4. Act as a catalyst for member participation in electronic networks.

GOAL 5.   **INFLUENCE CHANGE**

PALINET will influence libraries to embrace technological change.

Conditions
This goal addresses:

The need --
- For confidence in PALINET as a leader
- For libraries to incorporate technological change to provide quality, timely service to their users
- To influence change in order to deliver new services and products

The opportunity to --
- Forge effective partnerships
- Enhance PALINET's ability to serve as a change agent
- Move libraries into the future
- Further capitalize on PALINET's reputation as a trusted source of technological expertise

106

Strategies

1. Provide forums and showcases through which library management and staff increase their understanding of the potential benefit and value of technological change.
2. Create profiles of successful innovation in one or more libraries.
3. Develop and market products and services targeted to decision-makers and influencers (e.g., library directors, university presidents, school administrators, community officials) to increase support for effective change.
4. Seek to make change easier by providing comprehensive, integrated solutions for members and customers rather than just components.
5. Promote PALINET as a change agent.

#43 -- PALINET

BCR's Goals

1. BCR will be governed by a Board of Trustees which includes representatives of the broad interests of the members, provides a forum for the resolution of organizational issues and is open to and encouraging of the expression of the concerns of the membership.
2. BCR will encourage the participation of individuals from its member institutions in its organizational activities.
3. BCR will maintain its not-for-profit status.
4. BCR will maintain a financial condition that will allow the lowest possible pricing for products and services to its members while maintaining its ability to respond to future needs.
5. BCR will promote communication, cooperation and resource sharing among its members as well as with other library and information service institutions and organizations.
6. BCR will seek new members to enhance its base for cooperation and resource sharing.
7. BCR will market itself and its products and services to current and potential members.
8. BCR will offer products and services that will promote the effectiveness and efficiency of library and information organizations.
9. BCR will diversity its products and services in response to the changing needs of members, while maintaining high standards of quality and performance.
10. BCR will provide resources and a working environment that will support the development of staff.

#3 -- Bibliographical Center for Research, Rocky Mountain Regional, Inc.

Goals and Objectives

Facilitate the ability of libraries to provide timely, convenient, cost-effective access to information regardless of format, content, or location.

- Provide high quality information services that meet industry standards and convey a price advantage due to economies of scale available through AMIGOS membership.
- Provide libraries access to experts to support efficient, cost-effective integration and implementation of information systems.
- Inform members of information technology research initiatives to assist their technology decision-making.
- Assist libraries to develop programs that facilitate patron abilities to utilize emerging information technologies.

Assist libraries to play a leadership role in the information industry and in the development of national information policy.

- Promote awareness, among librarians and the broader information community, of the need for libraries to be active participants in national, regional, and state initiatives and policy decisions concerning information and telecommunications technology.
- Inform members of information industry standards development and provide services responsive to standards.
- Promote member awareness of information industry activities.

Aggressively develop, independently and in partnership with libraries and other information providers, new services for libraries and other consumers of information.

- Monitor information and telecommunication industries and pursue appropriate service development partnerships.
- Refine internal processes for identifying, assessing, and providing new services.
- Develop new services which enhance the information dissemination role of libraries.
- Focus on development and provision of services that help libraries go beyond bibliography to electronic provision of full text and imaging.
- Strengthen AMIGOS' role as a value-adding broker by working closely with OCLC and other partners in the development of end-user services.

Provide service to non-library entities and individuals in ways that support and enhance member library services.

- Explore development of a non-voting member category for non-library entities and individuals.
- Expand awareness of AMIGOS and its member libraries in non-library industries and among individual consumers.
- Explore expansion of services to the records management industry.

#1 -- AMIGOS

GOAL 1: All libraries are linked electronically.

1. Establish an electronic backbone which, by a local phone call or dedicated connection,. provides access to the world of information.
2. Set standards for connectivity and encourage dedicated access where practical.
3. Work with telecommunications providers to ensure reduced rates for libraries.
4. Establish an E-Mail system whereby all libraries may communicate with one another.

Implementation steps
- Utilize available expertise to aid in the development of a telecommunications plan.
- Contract with outside consultant/expert to review the telecommunications plan as needed.
- Provide funding for rewiring libraries.

GOAL 2: All libraries have the equipment to implement Libraries 2000.

1. Provide funding to equip each library with the hardware to get on the Internet.
2. Provide at least partial funding for connectivity costs.
3. Develop minimum standards for equipment purchases.

Implementation steps
- Provide funding (full or matching grants) to equip public libraries with state-of-the-art hardware for Internet access.
- Provide funding for other types of libraries as it becomes available.
- Form a committee to develop standards.
- Develop new grant programs and redesign existing programs to support equipment purchase. Permit libraries owning sufficient equipment to use grant funds for telecommunications costs.

GOAL 3: All libraries have Internet, World Wide Web Access.

1. Develop a list of Internet providers and guidelines for selection.
2. Negotiate for statewide Internet provider if practical.
3. Establish a network of telecommunications hub libraries and centers throughout the state to allow access to the Internet at a reasonable cost for smaller libraries.

Implementation steps
- Continue grant programs to fund telecommunications hub libraries.

GOAL 4: All libraries have access to an online bibliographic database and an interlibrary loan system.

1. Expand access to existing bibliographic databases and ILL systems.
2. Link existing bibliographic databases and ILL systems.
3. Develop statewide ILL system.

109

Implementation steps

- Continue to fund the Access Center to fill requests that cannot be filled elsewhere.
- Explore feasibility of implementing Z39.50 to search catalogs at multiple sites.
- Utilize the resources of small libraries as necessary through regional library catalogs.
- Continue to fund online access to the New Jersey Union List of Serials.

GOAL 5: All libraries have access to full text periodical articles and information in electronic formats.

1. Provide online access to basic full text periodical articles (1,000 titles minimum), sharing resources and responsibilities with local libraries and RLCs whenever possible.
2. Provide online access to specialized full text periodicals, with either state funding or a state match with local libraries or consortia.
3. Provide online access to full text reference sources.

Implementation steps

- Explore need for specialized resources and identify sources to meet those needs.
- Contract with vendors.

GOAL 6: All library staff have the expertise and skills to implement Libraries 2000.

1. Establish at least one training center in each of the four Network regions.
2. Identify needed skills.

Implementation steps

- Fund one training center for each Regional Library Cooperative.
- Continue support of "Train the Trainer" program.
- Identify additional funding necessary to implement training plans.
- Identify minimum competencies and develop training program based on these.
- Establish service hub libraries or centers to provide technical assistance to libraries.

#36 -- New Jersey State Library

SOUTH CAROLINA STATE LIBRARY
Goals and Objectives 1996-1997

Supplement to Strategic Plan 1996-1999

STRATEGIC GOAL A: PROVIDE INFORMATION RESOURCES AND SERVICES TO MEET THE NEEDS OF THE PEOPLE OF SOUTH CAROLINA

Goal 1. Serve as a partner with other libraries and information suppliers in providing information needed by South Carolinians in their daily lives.
Objectives:
- Develop a plan to expand access to State Library's Interlibrary Loan Service to all secondary schools in the state.
- Provide online access to the South Carolina Union List of Periodicals via the Internet.
- Provide online access to detailed holdings of the State Library's periodicals collection.
- Enhance the State Library's home page and encourage citizens, libraries, and state government employees to use it as an access point for information.
- Develop a pilot project for local libraries to access the State Library's Interlibrary Loan Service via the Internet.
- Update the SC Foundation Directory and provide online access.

Goal 2. Serve as the principal agent to advise, guide, and assist South Carolinians whose access to information is limited due to a disability which prevents the use of standard library formats.
Objectives:
- Develop a plan to make State Library databases accessible to both in-house and remote users who are unable to read computer screens due to a disability.
- Develop a mechanism for encouraging the use of adaptive technology in the development of home pages by state government agencies and South Carolina libraries.
- Develop and implement an action plan encouraging public libraries to promote the use of DBPH services.

Goal 3. Serve as the principal agent to advise, guide, and assist state government personnel in their quests for information.
Objectives:
- Investigate providing cataloging and database services for collections held by other state agencies.
- Develop methods for state government employees to place requests online.

#47 -- South Carolina State Library

SUMMARY OF GOALS

Goal 1:   Coordinated Leadership
The State Library of Florida and the Florida library community should establish the Florida Library Network Council to cooperatively plan for interlibrary cooperation, library resource sharing, and network development among Florida libraries.

Goal 2:   Continuing Education
Florida librarians should have access to coordinated continuing education opportunities to increase their ability to serve library users.

Goal 3:   Network Infrastructure
The FLNC should support expansion of the established statewide information networking infrastructure by collaborating in legislative efforts to recognize and more broadly define network applications and funding and by facilitating useful network connections for all types of Florida libraries, with the Internet as the "highway."

Goal 4:   Network Access and FLORANET
The extent of patron access to FLORANET networked information (and Internet resources) should be determined on the local level, by local libraries or Library Cooperatives, and by networks for their defined clientele, with general coordination and support provided by the State Library.

Goal 5:   Enhanced Network Content
The FLNC should support and encourage enhancement of bibliographic and information databases on FLORANET to include library holdings (public, private academic, and special libraries), commercial databases, state government information, access to public electronic networks, and selected Internet resources.

Goal 6:   Interlibrary Loan
Florida libraries should participate in a statewide Florida InterLibrary Loan (FILL) process to provide information and materials to Florida patrons.

Goal 7:   Reciprocal Borrowing
FLNC should develop a statewide reciprocal borrowing program in which Florida libraries should participate.

Goal 8:   Minimum Standards for Interlibrary Cooperation
The FLNC should develop minimum standards to serve as guidelines for resources needed to participate in the Florida Library Network.

Goal 9:   Preservation/Conservation
The FLNC should develop a plan for supporting preservation and conservation needs of Florida libraries, for both traditional and new technology materials, including disaster preparedness, professional education, sharing of remedial equipment, and patron access issues.

Goal 10:   Increased Public Awareness
The FLNC should develop a public awareness campaign to inform Florida residents of the benefits of their libraries' participation in the information highway.

All goals were developed by a participatory process that included focus groups with the Florida library community and discussion and recommendations from the Network Planning Task Force and the State Library of Florida staff.

GOALS AND RESPONSIBILITIES

Goal 1: Coordinated Leadership

The State Library of Florida and the Florida library community should establish the Florida Library Network Council to cooperatively plan for interlibrary cooperation, library resource sharing, and network development among Florida libraries.

There is a critical need for coordination of interlibrary cooperation, resource sharing, and network development among Florida libraries. Some groups of libraries are already organized and making their resources available online (FCLA, CCLA, SEFLIN, TBLC); others are in the planning stages for online access (SUNLINK); others have their holdings in machine readable format but not accessible outside their library building; and still others have not yet begun the automation process.

Florida libraries are at a critical juncture where they can move forward with a network that allows maximum access to the resources of all Florida libraries through simple electronic interfaces. Planning and coordination of this access must begin now.

The Florida Library Network Council (FLNC) would serve as the coordinating body and would have as participants the major stakeholders in library resource sharing and network development. The FLNC would be composed of representatives from groups who have accepted or been assigned responsibility for network development in Florida. The FLNC will have two major responsibilities:

1) The FLNC will cooperatively plan for resource sharing and network development in Florida of both electronic and non-electronic activities. The resulting plans would give direction to all the FLNC members as they plan their own resource sharing and networking activities. FLNC members would have the ability and responsibility to represent their constituents and members. FLNC members would be asked to commit the resources of their organization or members or be able and willing to encourage members to move forward on statewide network plans.

2) The FLNC will advise the State Library of Florida on needed actions and the allocation of resources to further the *Florida Plan for Interlibrary Cooperation, Resource Sharing, and Network Development.*

113

Membership in FLNC

The interests of following groups would be represented on FLNC:

CCLA (College Center for Library Automation)
CFLC (Central Florida Library Consortium)
FCLA (Florida Center for Library Automation)
FIRN (Florida Information Resource Network)
NEFLIN (Northeast Florida Library Information Network)
PLAN (Panhandle Library Access Network)
SEFLIN (SouthEast Florida Library Information Network)
SUNLINK (School Library Media Network)
SWFLN (Southwest Florida Library Network)
TBLC (Tampa Bay Library Consortium)
Special libraries
State University System libraries
Private academic libraries
Community college libraries
Public libraries
School library media centers
State information stakeholders
     University of South Florida Library School
     Florida State University School of Library and Information Studies
     Joint Committee on Information Technology Resources
     Information Resource Commission
     Division of Communications
State Library of Florida

Networks would be asked to select their representative to FLNC. Type of library representatives would be chosen by the State Library based on recommendations or nominations. An effort would be made to make certain that all geographic areas are represented, as well as libraries that are not in Library Cooperatives and whose collections are not yet accessible electronically. Membership would be reviewed periodically to ensure that all key stakeholders, such as new Library Cooperatives, continue to be represented.

In order to be most effective, the FLNC should meet as needed with subgroups working between meetings in order to accomplish the work of the Council. Participating groups will be asked to provide financial support for their representatives' attendance at necessary meetings.

The chair of the FLNC should be the State Librarian. The State Library should also have a participating, voting member to ensure the State Library concerns are represented in all discussions. Staff administrative assistance (agendas, meeting arrangements, etc.) should be provided by the State Library.

FLNC and its members should communicate regularly with the library community about issues under discussion, decisions made, and documents produced. FLNC should take advantage of the strengths of larger libraries of all types as it identifies and uses resources to fill gaps in statewide library service.

Responsibilities for action will rest on all the participants in the FLNC. Each will have a role to play, and successful resource sharing and network development will depend on the acceptance of this responsibility, coordinated planning, and commitment to action.

Responsibilities for Goal 1

FLNC	State Library	Library Cooperatives and Networks	Local libraries
Advise the State Library on resource sharing goals, network development, and the allocation of resources	Coordinate the activity of the FLNC. Provide staff assistance in facilitating the work of the FLNC	Gather input from constituents on resource sharing needs and willingness to participate in statewide plans	Share information about needs and resources available for resource sharing and network development in Florida
Cooperatively plan with the State Library and each other for resource sharing and network development	Obtain input from the FLNC on State Library plans for interlibrary cooperation, resource sharing, and network development in Florida	Represent users needs and commitments to the FLNC	Participate in statewide and regional resource sharing activities
Commit resources of member organizations where possible	Take a leadership role in implementing network plans statewide	Take a leadership role in implementing the goals of the Resource Sharing/Network Development Plan	Financially support FLNC when and if necessary
Encourage participation in network plans by member's constituents	Encourage all libraries in Florida to participate in resource sharing and network development	Financially support FLNC when and if necessary	Assist in publicizing activities of FLNC to constituents
Assist in publicizing the activities of FLNC to constituents	Assist in publicizing the activities of the FLNC to Florida libraries	Assist in publicizing the activities of FLNC to constituents	
Financially support FLNC when and if necessary			
Attend meetings and participate			

#17 -- Florida Network Planning Task Force and the State Library of Florida

115

Goal 3: Facilitate the sharing of resources, information, expertise, and cooperative opportunities to all Nebraskans through libraries and networked electronic services.

Genesis: Resource sharing programs and services have a long history of development in Nebraska whether focused towards paper or electronic exchange of information. The Library Commission's support of interlibrary loan began with the building of a statewide Union Catalog (listing book holdings for major libraries in the state) in the 1930s, as part of a WPA project. The Commission has also supported location of serials through maintenance of the Nebraska Union List of Serials Titles (NEULIST) which has also changed and developed over the past years as the technological capabilities of member libraries has increased.

The current priorities and guidelines for use of Library Services and Construction Act funds also target resource sharing and technological activities. In addition, the *1989 Strategic Plan* and the *1990 Resource Sharing Review Final Report* have enabled the Commission to sharpen its focus in these areas, with the active participation of libraries and key stakeholders within the state.

Resource sharing of government documents is carried out through the state and federal depository library programs. In 1972 the Nebraska Publications Clearinghouse was created at the NLC, with statutory authority to collect all Nebraska state documents and distribute them to depository libraries across the state.

Continue support and development of *Nebrask@ Online*, in cooperation with the Nebraska Development Network, based on the Memo of Understanding with the Rural Development Commission, which includes the Goal, Objectives, and Provisions (October 29, 1991).

Needs: Nebraska ranks 10th among the states in the number of public libraries. The majority of these libraries are in communities of under 1,500 population. These many small community libraries, and the many smaller rural communities in Nebraska, do not have budgets which allow the acquisition of sufficient library materials to serve the varied needs of the people in these communities. Cooperative programs are needed to share library resources among the libraries of the state.

In this information age, no library can serve all the information needs of its users from its own physical resources. Resource sharing, document delivery, and provision of electronic access to networks makes materials, expertise, and a wide variety of information available to all citizens. The Commission struggles to minimize the effects of geographic and economic disparities upon localities' access to resources and information. Interagency cooperation, technology, and networking play major roles in this endeavor.

It is the intent of Network Services, of the Library Commission, to promote and support libraries in their cooperative efforts to share resources and information. Network Services will:
- assist librarians in delivering information to Nebraska citizens through electronic exchange;
- develop and support access to state government information resources, and to national and international communications networks; introduce and promote new products that assist member libraries to use information technologies;

116

- provide cost-effective, innovative training to strengthen libraries in the use of information technologies;
- support and enhance member library programs which promote regional cooperation and resource sharing.

Operation of NEBASE, the statewide OCLC network, is supported largely through state funds, with supplemental funding for specific services provided through LSCA Title III. The development and maintenance of a shared bibliographical database is necessary for the identification, location, and interlibrary loan of library materials. The OCLC network is critical in a large state with many rural communities. This network and related cooperative agreements allow smaller libraries to access the resources of other libraries to meet the information needs of people in their communities. This multitype library network connects public, academic, school, and special libraries so they can share their unique resources.

Nebrask@ Online and the Internet, online databases, as well as other computer-aided information retrieval services, allow libraries the means to find needed information: In addition, *Nebrask@ Online* will provide Internet access for libraries with no local provider. The resources available to those with access include large commercial databases which typically charge for access to smaller, more specialized services which may be publicly supported. Many libraries lack the funds and skilled personnel to directly access these services. Cooperative arrangements and an increased emphasis on building libraries' autonomy facilitates access to and delivery of this information to people throughout Nebraska.

For the past 11 years, the Commission has supported six library systems which have assumed responsibility for contracting for interlibrary loan and reference services for libraries which are not direct participants in the NEBASE network. As a result of the 1993 review of the regional library system program, the Resource Sharing Advisory Committee along with representatives of the regional library systems continues to meet and work toward a more consistent statewide approach to interlibrary loan and reference services.

Under the Major Urban Resources provisions of the Library Services and Construction Act Title I, funds are provided to the Lincoln and Omaha Public Libraries. These funds are allocated for collection development and equipment to enhance the urban libraries' role as resource centers for other Nebraska libraries. Access to materials and information provided by the Omaha Public Library and the Lincoln City Libraries assists other public libraries in providing service to their communities.

The Consumer Health Information Resource Service (CHIRS), provided through the University of Nebraska Medical Center, offers information materials to the public through public libraries. Public library clients can acquire health information materials through their local library, or they can borrow materials through CHIRS. This program has become a model for providing public access to support personal health information needs.

Objectives:

3.1   Administer and provide services to Nebraska libraries offered by NEBASE, the statewide OCLC (Online Computer Library Center, Inc.) network. Support continued development of the shared state database which is a subset of the 32 million record international OCLC database.

Evaluation:
- Analyze usage reports provided by OCLC.
- Document support calls to Library Commission staff.
- Provide training in use of OCLC products. Evaluation forms will be completed by participants. Participants will also be asked to name additional training they feel should be offered.
- NEBASE annual meeting will be held in more than one location.
- NEBASE advisory council will meet quarterly to provide input on NEBASE services.
- N3 (N-cubed), NEBASE services newsletter, will be published six times a year.

3.2   Support application of technology to improve local service.

Evaluation:
- Provide training in use of the Internet for reference and information services.
- Provide training, as identified, for other electronic information sources.
- Maintain the web sites for the Nebraska Library Commission and the Nebraska State Government home pages.

3.3   Promote cooperation among libraries in Nebraska for resource sharing.

Evaluation:
- Promote LVIS (Libraries Very Interested in Sharing), number of libraries signing the LVIS agreement in 1997-1999.
- Number of libraries participating in resource sharing in 1997-1999.
- Number of items loaned during 1997-1999.
- Retain and compile comments received from patrons concerning how the service made a difference to their lives.

3.4   Distribute federal LSCA funding, according to federal requirements, to Lincoln and Omaha Public Libraries under the MURLS program.

Evaluation: Gather and report data regarding the distribution and use of MURLS funds, and the impact of those funds upon the major urban libraries and upon statewide resource sharing.

3.5   Continue development and operation of *Nebrask@ Online* for convenient, timely, and efficient online access to state government information.

#32 -- Nebraska Library Commission

STRATEGIC GOALS

1. Facilitate implementation of a virtual statewide database of library holdings (individual library holdings databases linked to form a distributed database) and information that includes circulation status and access policies and reduces the barriers to borrowing and disseminating materials among libraries.

The role of the Council of Wisconsin Libraries, as a statewide multitype organization, is to identify leading edge developments within the library community and to encourage and facilitate other libraries following this lead. The Wisconsin library community is moving toward a virtual statewide database with development of shared automated systems, and/or systems with Z39.50 capability, so that libraries can more easily share resources within a broad community. At the beginning of 1995 there are at least seven shared systems either fully operational or under development, including nearly seventy-five public, academic and technical college libraries. Wisconsin's leading edge libraries have set the direction and pace; COWL must now communicate the vision and facilitate its implementation.

2. Facilitate statewide access for library users to information/reference services and expertise through any library location in the State; coordinate statewide licensing arrangements with vendors of electronic information; if appropriate, negotiate licenses and/or arrange for central or regional access to electronic databases for Wisconsin users.

A virtual database is only one component of the virtual library that is in Wisconsin's future. Wisconsin library users must also have access to reference and information services that extend beyond the limitations of any one library. The virtual Wisconsin library must include all types of materials and information including materials in electronic formats. In reality, electronic information has the greatest potential for resource sharing, and advances in telecommunication such as the Internet have provided the vehicle through which sharing can occur. COWL has an opportunity and obligation to serve a coordination role in making such services and licensing arrangements accessible to all Wisconsin libraries.

3. Improve the efficiency, cost effectiveness, and accessibility of interlibrary loan and document delivery through the coordination and/or development of statewide courier/delivery options, and policies to move library resources between and among Wisconsin libraries.

Wisconsin has a tradition of very structured and relatively efficient intrastate interlibrary loan. The State Library Agency and its public library systems provide direct service and coordinate interloan for public and school libraries; COWL, through WILS, provides direct service and serves as the access point to the State's academic library resources. A virtual database will improve access to the State's library resources, but without equivalent improvements in lending processes and turn-around-time for delivery of materials and information to patrons, the database will not reach its full potential. In addition, COWL must assist libraries in acquiring and/or reallocating funds to support the costs of sharing materials and information. Wisconsin libraries and their governing bodies must understand the costs and benefits of resource sharing and must make a commitment to participate in the state sharing network through the maintenance of strong local collections and the allocation of adequate resource to support the costs of sharing materials and information with other libraries.

4. Assure participation of Wisconsin libraries in emerging community networks as suppliers, producers, and users of electronic information.

The essence of community networking is the application of technology to enhance access to local information. Providing public access to local information is a long-standing role of libraries; whether it is making government documents available, collecting city and county records for public review, or serving as a referral source for community service, libraries have been a primary resource. As services become electronic through the emergence of community networks it is critical that libraries continue to be key players.

5. Coordinate, develop, or facilitate the development of, programs to assist libraries in providing user education to facilitate their role in teaching information-seeking skills to their users. Coordinate staff development programs for libraries, including technical support and training for libraries in accessing electronic resources, and assistance for libraries in meeting the challenges of providing services to distance learners.

The new world of libraries and information services necessitates a new way of thinking and of providing service for those who work in libraries. Librarians are being called upon to train and assist users in accessing electronic information both within and far beyond the traditional library collection. COWL must take an active role in the area of staff development to ensure that librarians have the tools and knowledge they need to meet such demands.

6. Communicate to funding agencies and the citizenry of Wisconsin the societal, economic, cultural and educational value of libraries and promote the vision of libraries as an essential interface between people and information.

While libraries have never really been adequately funded, the financial resources of Wisconsin's libraries will be even more severely limited in the foreseeable future. The infrastructure of major resource collections cannot be weakened if resource sharing is to continue and be strengthened.

In addition to real funding cuts and decreases in buying power, libraries are also seeing their role and value questioned due to the perceptions of the "information highway" development. As a corporate organization of libraries COWL has an obligation towards the future welfare and development of the institutions it represents.

STRATEGIC ACTION PLAN & TIMETABLE

The Action Plan is designed to address the six Strategic Goals concurrently through the involvement of COWL, specially appointed COWL Committees, and the COWL service program staff (WILS). Actions are specified for the first three fiscal (July-June) years. Actions for years four and five will be developed as implementation of the Strategic Plan proceeds.

Goal 1
Facilitate implementation of a virtual statewide database of library holdings and information that includes circulation status and access policies and reduces the barriers to borrowing and disseminating materials among libraries.

ACTION

Communicate the COWL vision of "combined resources of the libraries in Wisconsin that are accessible and available to the people of Wisconsin," and the development of a virtual statewide database as the means to achieve the vision, to gain acceptance and commitment within the Wisconsin library community by the end of fiscal '96.

(a) As an organization composed of representatives of the various library communities, COWL is well positioned to communicate its vision throughout the State. COWL members will, in fiscal '96, present and discuss the Resource Sharing Vision Statement & Strategic Goals with their constituencies. Reactions, ideas and issues of concern will be brought to the full COWL Board for consideration. The goal will be to gain statewide acceptance of the vision and a commitment to work towards making the vision a reality.

(b) To facilitate statewide consensus on the Vision and Strategic Goals COWL will sponsor programs and publications on the evolution to a virtual library. Programs may be planned in cooperation with WLA-related conferences; publications will not necessarily be original writing but rather a "contents alert" type of service to call attention to articles and/or related programs through WISlib, the WILS electronic discussion group for Wisconsin.

#15 -- Council of Wisconsin Libraries, Inc.

Strategy I: Provide Quality Information Services

We intend to move further in the direction of a library driven by customer demand and the customer's need to cope with information overload. Such a change is necessary to provide quality information services to those in state government who may not have enough time to know what information is available, let alone learn how to obtain it. In all its efforts, the State Library will assist the people of California in gaining electronic access to the information resources of state government.

STRATEGY 1.1 REASSESS AND REALIGN LIBRARY SERVICES

ISSUE   *A dynamic economic, political and technological environment demands that we stay in touch with and position ourselves to respond to the rapidly changing information needs of both state government and the public.*

GOALS   Reassess customer needs for timeliness, convenience, and delivery methods for information services.

                Realign library services as suggested by changing needs of customers.

STRATEGY 1.2 MAXIMIZE TECHNOLOGY PARTNERSHIPS

ISSUE   *Rapidly changing technology, coupled with increasing costs and continuing competition for scarce public and private resources, requires that we optimize partnerships in order to maximize our investments in technology and to develop and achieve our shared objectives.*

GOALS   Help make state and local agency information available on the Internet.

                Promote effective public and state agency use of the resources of the Internet by working with libraries and agency partners to identify and/or develop training and navigational tools.

                Develop strategic partnerships to ensure that public libraries are included at the policy level in the evolving national information infrastructure.

                Continue to provide leadership and support for the InFoPeople (public library Internet access) initiative.

#6 -- California State Library

GOAL # 1

To provide New Hampshire residents the benefits of improved interlibrary cooperation and resource sharing through the increased capacity of the New Hampshire Automated Information System and the application of developing informational technologies.

OBJECTIVE 1.1

To provide New Hampshire residents access to state, regional, national, and international information resources.

RATIONALE

No one library can meet all of the information needs of its clients from its own collection. Advances in information technology have made the "library without walls" possible.

RECOMMENDED ACTION

Task 1 -- State Library

> Coordinate the preparation of a plan for the development of a statewide education telecommunications backbone to involve the University System of New Hampshire, the Department of Education, the Department of Postsecondary Education, and the Department of Cultural Affairs. Completion date: 12/92

Task 2 --.State Library

> Replace the existing NHAIS telecommunications network with access to T-1 telephone lines, existing high speed modems with 9600 baud variable rate modems, and upgrade other equipment to support digital transmission of large documents and multimedia formats. Completion date: 6/94

Task 3 -- State Library

> Secure Internet address space so that all libraries can access the Internet. Completion date: 12/92

Task 4 -- State Library

> Identify existing state databases that could and should be accessed through the network. Completion date: ongoing

Task 5 -- State Library

> Develop the capacity to access CD-ROM data files through the network. Completion date: 3/93

Task 6 -- State Library

> Develop a Library Techniques course dealing with the use and applications of networked library resources. Completion date: 1/93

Task 7 -- State Library

> Develop workshops for library staffs on the use of NHAIS and the Internet. Completion date: 6/93

Task 8 -- State Library

> Revise and update the NHAIS User's Manual. Completion date: 12/92

Task 9 -- Local Libraries

> All libraries to budget funds for local access to NHAIS. Completion date: 12/96

Task 10 -- Local Libraries

> Promote the use of NHAIS locally. Completion date: ongoing

Task 11 -- Local Libraries

> Provide time for staff to attend workshops and training opportunities on the use of networked library resources. Completion date: ongoing

Task 12 -- NHAIS Board
Explore the acquisition of licensing agreements to load commercially available databases onto the network. Completion date: 3/93

OBJECTIVE 1.2
To provide efficient and timely exchange of information and enhance networking among libraries of all types.

RATIONALE
Libraries must be able to easily locate, request, and receive requested materials in a time frame consistent with the clients' needs or they will by-pass the library and seek the material elsewhere.

RECOMMENDED ACTION
Task 1 -- State Library
Provide statewide electronic mail and interlibrary loan. Completion date: 6/94
Task 2 -- State Library
Coordinate and encourage the drafting and implementation of cooperative collection development policies. Completion date: ongoing
Task 3 -- State Library
Develop the capacity to provide full-text document delivery between libraries and clients. Completion date: 9/94
Task 4 -- State Library
Establish standards for database creation, connectivity, and data exchange. Completion date: Initially 9/92; then as needed
Task 5 -- State Library
Encourage the development of cooperative local automated systems when such systems will provide greater access to information and enhance interlibrary cooperation. Completion date: ongoing
Task 6 -- Local Libraries
Register and use the electronic mail and interlibrary loan systems available through NHAIS. Completion date: all libraries by 1/2000
Task 7 -- Local Libraries
Acquire software and hardware necessary to receive digitized full text documents through NHAIS. Completion date: all libraries by 1/2000
Task 8 -- Local Libraries
Adhere to standards for database creation, connectivity, and data exchange. Completion date: 12/92
Task 9 -- Local Libraries
Require all library automation vendors to adhere to standards when securing local automation products and services. Completion date: 12/92
Task 10 -- Local Systems/Cooperatives
Establish user groups to deal with technical issues, build competence in using the system, etc. Completion date: ongoing
Task 11 -- Local Systems/Cooperatives
Form cooperative automated networks when greater benefits can be achieved. Completion date: ongoing

#35 -- New Hampshire State Library

124

Meridian Library System
1995-1997 SYSTEM STRATEGIC PLAN

Goal 1: To provide consulting services to library and media center personnel.
     Objectives:

     A. To provide information on such basic library skills as collection development, weeding, and grant writing. This objective will be implemented by the following action steps:

1. To encourage the use of jobbers by System libraries through publishing an annual article in the newsletter.
2. To assist at least five libraries annually in the evaluation and improvement of the local collection.
3. To offer at least one workshop or workshop component on collection development each year.

     B. To provide problem resolution. The System Administrator will be available for consultation and facilitation of conflict. Priority will be given to schools and media centers in the following order: public libraries, special libraries, school media centers, college/university libraries.

     C. To provide basic education and encouragement so system libraries and media centers can make effective and efficient use of library resources through automation and telecommunication development. This objective will be implemented by the following action steps:

1. To offer at least one workshop component on technology each year.
2. To offer names of technical support people.
3. To provide the services of a technical support person for basic technology instruction.

Goal 2: To aid system libraries and media centers in providing for the full range of patron information needs through access to an interlibrary loan center and a reference center.
     Objectives:

     A. To provide interlibrary loan service through the System's contractual arrangement. This objective will be implemented by the following action steps:

1. Provide interlibrary loan center information to all member libraries and media centers.
2. Provide publicity and promotion via System newsletter and brochures.

     B. To provide secondary level reference service through the System's contractual arrangement. This objective will be implemented by the following action steps:

1. Provide reference center information to all member libraries and media centers.
2. Provide publicity and promotion via System newsletter and brochures.

C. To provide access to large print materials through the System's contractual arrangement. This objective will be implemented by the following action steps:
1. Provide information on large print materials service to all member libraries and media centers.
2. Provide publicity and promotion via System newsletter and brochures.
3. Provide $500 grant annually for purchase of large print materials.
4. Publish additions to the collections once a year in the newsletter.

Goal 3: To aid library and media center personnel to increase the scope of their knowledge about library practice and technologies.
Objectives:
A. To present at least four workshops annually to a total audience of at least 100 persons (including at least 20 participants from school library media centers).
B. To continue to offer a professional materials collection. This objective will be implemented by adding at least five new items to the collection each year.
C. To have two persons attend System or state sponsored programs that will increase professional competence. This objective will be implemented by offering scholarships for attendance at professional growth programs.
D. To provide orientation for new system library board members.

Goal 4: Library and media center personnel are well-informed about system services.
Objectives:
A. To emphasize a System service once each year in the newsletter.
B. To visit 85% of the library/media centers in the System every two years.
C. To conduct Board meetings in at least three different System locations annually.
D. To update promotional materials biennially. This objective will be implemented by the following action steps:
1. Prepare updated brochure during first quarter of every other year.
2. Update System directory by end of each calendar year.
3. Publish System newsletter ten months a year.

Goal 5: To aid system libraries and media centers in providing enhanced service to children and youth through workshops and grants.
Objectives:
A. To increase by 50% the number of libraries providing special programming to children and youth. This objective will be implemented by the following action steps:
1. Presenting at least two workshops annually focusing on services to children and youth.
2. Publishing lists of recommended materials in the newsletter.
3. Providing four grants each year to system libraries for programs to children and youth.

#28 -- Meridian Library System

GOAL 1

Services
Maximize citizens' access to information through automated systems.

OBJECTIVES
- Provide shared circulation system for all members.
- Provide shared on-line catalog for all members.
- Provide access for disabled users.
- Develop shared acquisitions system to the extent possible.
- Implement integrated acquisitions and serials control software compatible with existing system.
- Expand database to include all materials held by participating libraries (Government publications, archival materials, audiovisual, serials, etc.)
- Coordinate collection development using the system to allow for more effective materials expenditures.
- Provide self-service checkout/in stations to facilitate client privacy and staff efficiency.
- Provide access to a broad range of bibliographic and full-text databases.
- Provide efficient, economical/access to databases used to build local files and retrieve non-locally held information.

GOAL 2

Staffing
Provide adequate staff to manage the CLAN network.

OBJECTIVES
- Restore State Library staff assistance for systems operation through state funds.
- Dedicate CLAN-funded position to computer operations.

GOAL 3

Training
Assure availability of state-of-the-art training for all CLAN participants.

OBJECTIVES
- Provide regular training opportunities for CLAN coordinator and systems operator.
- Provide quarterly training workshops for all CLAN members.
- Train NSLA personnel as back-up computer operators.

GOAL 4

Funding
Provide a stable funding base from a variety of sources.

OBJECTIVES
- Fund all central site operational costs through participant fees.
- Fund local hardware and operations through local financial sources.
- Develop a capital improvements fund through local, state and private sources.
- Match capital improvement funds with federal Library Services and Construction Act funds.

GOAL 5

Hardware/Software
Provide reliable and efficient hardware and software to meet user needs.

OBJECTIVES
- Establish minimum standards for local hardware and software to ensure network compatibility.
- Support open systems architecture as required by State standards adopted by Department of Data Processing.
- Develop methods to evaluate members grant and other funding requests.
- Implement user-end backup system.
- Upgrade central site hardware to meet end-user requirements including disk storage, database backup and ininterruptible power supply.
- Upgrade central site software to meet end-user requirements including database searching, dial in serials access and single user back-up software.

GOAL 6

Database Access
**Provide efficient economical access to databases used to build local files
and retrieve non-locally held information.**

OBJECTIVES
- Implement bibliographic database services to provide immediate updates to CLSI via direct interface.
- Explore alternative back-up catalogs compatible with existing or upgradable user equipment.
- Integrate local, network wide and statewide databases on CLSI system to provide users a single source to a wide variety of information.
- Evaluate online full-text access to indexes and periodicals to provide public access to licensed databases from a single source.
- Provide access to databases available through NREN, Internet, etc.

GOAL 7

Handicapped
Provide access for handicapped users through use of new technologies.

OBJECTIVES

- Meet requirements of American Disabilities Act by providing voice catalogs; large viewing screens, CCTV; braille output, etc.

GOAL 8

Telecommunications
Manage telecommunications network which provides efficient access to all shared databases.

OBJECTIVES

- Manage all telecommunications requirements to ensure compatibility and adherence to the plan.
- Keep abreast of all state plans regarding telecommunications which could impact services.
- Reevaluate existing network structure.
- Provide FAX modems with scanners to ensure efficient, timely public access.
- Add routers, bridges, or gateways to provide local access to remote databases, local and/or wide area networks.
- Enhance accessibility at the local or state levels through telecommunications servers, modem pool processor cards, etc.
- Add network manager system operating computer to efficiently help resolve network problems and network security.

#34 d. -- Nevada State Library & Archives

NETWORK SERVICE GOALS: An Overview

Goal 1: Information Access

Through the Network, end users will have the benefit of integrated statewide resource sharing systems by which to identify, access and retrieve needed information resources.

To achieve this goal by the end of 1996, the Network will:

1.1: Support public access to the Internet and provide guidance in the use of the electronic superhighway.

1.2: Strengthen the interlibrary loan capabilities of member libraries in order that end users can secure needed information and resources not available at their local library.

1.3: Coordinate timely, cost-effective delivery of information and materials through physical and electronic means.

1.4: Provide member libraries assistance in meeting the general and specialized information retrieval and reference needs of end users.

1.5: Achieve a statewide library borrowing program that allows all users to have access to materials and information regardless of where they live or where the material is located.

1.6: Expand distance learning opportunities available to end users.

1.7: Promote end user education to assure efficient use of Network services and access to the collective resources of the membership.

Goal 2: Resource Development

The Network will enhance the ability of member libraries to contribute to, and participate in, local, state and national resource sharing initiatives.

To achieve this goal by the end of 1996, the Network will:

2.1: Provide ways by which member libraries can identify and gain access to resources held by Indiana libraries through their contributions to, and participation in, state database development.

2.2: Act as a stimulus for the development of community "freenets."

2.3: Educate and train librarians and support staff to act as intermediaries in connecting end users to local, state and global information resources -- and to use appropriate information technologies.

2.4: Promote the availability of distance learning opportunities for library personnel statewide.

2.5: Provide consultation and mentoring services to facilitate member library participation in resource sharing, the adoption of new technologies, and the use of network programs and services.

2.6: Develop, manage and evaluate appropriate cooperative contracting and procurement opportunities for the membership in order to save money, promote cooperative projects, and use resources more effectively.

Goal 3: Network Development

The Network will conduct research and participate in planning to improve information access and to further information resource development.

To achieve this goal by the end of 1996, the Network will:

3.1: Sponsor market research and participate in planning in order to target priority network services for end users and member libraries.

3.2: Plan for network development and assist with statewide planning through collaboration with end users and representatives from member libraries and other agencies.

3.3: Promote the use of new technologies which demonstrate promise for improving state resource sharing programs.

3.4: Promote the development of state, national, and international standards and guidelines and work to promote their use within the Network.

3.5: Participate in the development of state and national information policy.

3.6: Act as an advocate for libraries and end users at the local, state and national levels.

3.7: Cultivate information partnerships with libraries and civic, business, education and government groups.

#21 -- Indiana State Library

VIRTUAL NETWORK PARTNERS -- ROLES AND RESPONSIBILITIES

	State Library	The Network	Network Members
Service Delivery Roles	Provides consulting and continuing education opportunities to libraries in coordination with the Network.	Carries out goals & objectives set forth in the Network Plan for Service.	Participate in network activities and programs.
	Provides library service to state government as well as services to the handicapped as the state regional library for the blind.	Provides network services to member libraries.	Provide library service to library patrons and information users.
Policy Development & Implementation Roles	Establishes policy for use of state and federal funds.	Provides opportunities for members to set network policies through their representation on 3 types of advisory councils.	Participate in policy discussions at the state and network levels and set local policy.
	Establishes official standards via the authority of the Indiana Library and Historical Board.	Participates in setting state policy & standards through COLA, ISLAC, and the Network Coordinating Council.	Follow state policies and standards in providing library service.
Budgetary and Funding Roles	Requests state funds for the network through state budget process. Assists with advocating for funding. Administers LSCA funds.	Establishes yearly budget request to support service plan goals & objectives.	Advocate for funding with legislature and approve yearly network budget for transmittal to the State Library.
Partnering Roles	Provides liaison to state government initiatives.	Partners with appropriate outside groups in providing services.	Recommend possible networking partners.

132

	State Library	The Network	Network Members
Planning Roles	Develops statewide plan for library development. Participates in network planning through Network Coordinating Council.	Develops the network plan for service.	Participate in network planning through three types of Network Advisory Councils.
Regulatory and Oversight Roles	Assesses accountability for state & federal funds. Collects library statistics. Reviews and approves LSA budget request & plan. Monitors compliance with standards.	Develops standards for accountability.	Provide statistical information to the State Library. Report on compliance with standards.

#21 -- Indiana State Library

133

North Country Reference and Research Resources Council
Plan of Development 1996 - 2000

Goals/ Objectives/Activities/Tasks	Target Year/Years					Target Completion Date	Position/Committee Responsible
	1996	1997	1998	1999	2000		
I. COUNCIL GOAL FOR ELECTRONIC/ BIBLIOGRAPHIC ACCESS AND CONTROL: Researchers, students, teachers and the general public will have enhanced access to electronic, bibliographic and other informational resources both within and outside the North Country as the result of NC3R'S Council activities.							
1. Citizens will have prompt access to regional resources.	X	X	X	X	X	On-going	Executive Director
a. Develop/review strategies for consolidating access to all regional bibliographic records and holdings statements.	X	X	X			December, 1997	NC3R'S Staff/Auto. Comm.
b. Encourage end-user access to all regional bibliographic records and holdings statements.	X	X	X	X	X	On-going	NC3R'S Staff/Auto. Comm
i. Provide libraries within the region with public access related equipment at subsidized or no cost.	X	X	X			December, 1998	NC3R'S Staff/Auto. Comm.
ii. Continue to provide public access library NorthNet accounts.	X	X	X	X	X	On-going	NC3R'S Staff/Auto. Comm.

North Country Reference and Research Resources Council
Plan of Development 1996 - 2000

Goals/ Objectives/Activities/Tasks	Target Year/Years					Target Completion Date	Position/Committee Responsible
	1996	1997	1998	1999	2000		
c. Continue expansion, publication, and distribution of NORPAC (presently on CD-ROM).	X	X	X			December, 1998	NC3R's Staff/Auto. Comm.
d. Continue to offer Group Access Capability and monitor use.	X	X				December, 1997	NC3R'S Staff/Auto. Comm.
e. Continue retrospective bibliographic conversion of regional holdings with the goal of completion before 1999.	X	X	X	X		December, 1999	NC3R'S Staff/ Auto. Comm.
ii. Investigate costs and strategies for converting remaining collections of significance (manuscripts, gov't documents, local history, A-V materials).	X	X	X	X		December, 1999	NC3R'S Staff/Auto. Comm.
2. Citizens will have prompt access to non-regional resources.	X	X	X	X	X	On-going	Executive Director
a. Pursue opportunities for fee based information services to business, industry and government.	X	X				December, 1997	NC3R'S Staff
b. Continue to vend NorthNet access and services beyond the library community, and monitor usage on system.	X	X	X	X	X	On-going	NC3R'S Staff/Automation Committee

#38 -- North County Reference & Research Resources Council

GOAL 2: Continuing Education

Coordinated opportunities for continuing education will be provided to increase library staff's ability to serve library users.

Objective 1. Determine the continuing education needs of member libraries and convey those needs to a continuing education coordinating group.

Objective 2. Offer continuing education activities to meet member needs.

Objective 3. Work cooperatively with USF's School of Library and Information Science to increase library training opportunities for the state

Objective 4. Arrange for the reception of remote learning services.

Background:

TBLC has become an important part of Florida's library education infrastructure. Through Member requests gathered from such instruments such as surveys, evaluations, and electronic conferencing notes, TBLC continues to develop workshops that meet our Member's needs. In 1994/1995 the consortium provided 70 workshops to over 1000 attendees. This makes TBLC the largest library continuing education provider in Florida.

One unique feature of regional consortium education is that knowledge and skills found within our own geographic area are able to be used and shared. While primarily providing learning opportunities, at the same time, this is also providing teaching opportunities. Many professionals have been able to turn these occasions for teaching at TBLC into leadership and teaching roles at state and national conferences.

CONTINUING EDUCATION ONGOING ACTION PLANS 1995/96 through 1999/00

TIMELINE	ACTION PLAN	RESPONSIBILITY
August	Revise and distribute to TBLC area professionals and support staff a continuing education needs assessment	Associate Director
September	Analyze survey data and report it to the TBLC Continuing Education Committee	Associate Director
October	Finalize Continuing Education recommendations and present them to TBLC staff and Board	Associate Director
Annually	Set TBLC's continuing education priorities using the TBLC Continuing Education survey as a guide	Continuing Education Committee
Throughout the year	Develop, coordinate, implement and sponsor continuing education activities for library professionals, paraprofessionals and other support staff	Associate Director
Throughout the year	Produce a quarterly schedule of workshop activities based on member input	Associate Director and TBLC staff
Throughout the year	Work cooperatively with USF's School of Library and Information Science to increase library training opportunities	Executive Director/ Associate Director
Throughout the year	Provide access to a computer training room with a least 20 workstations	Associate Director
Throughout the year	Identify TBLC Member Library staff that are willing to share their expertise by teaching workshops	Associate Director
Throughout the year	Develop training programs for select subject areas as determined by the continuing education needs assessment. Include hands on electronic access and resources	Associate Director
Throughout the year	Coordinate CE with the USF School of Library and Information Science's Director and continuing education liaison	Associate Director
Throughout the year	Work with the Director and staff of the University of South Florida's Library School to provide workshops that are of interest to both students and faculties	Executive Director/ Associate Director
Throughout the year	Coordinate with USF's School of Library and Information Science to use their facilities, especially for workshops requiring state-of-the-art technology	Associate Director
Throughout the year	Share teaching expertise, especially in library technology and resource sharing with USF's School of Library and Information Science.	Associate Director

137

CONTINUING EDUCATION ONGOING ACTION PLANS 1995/96 through 1999/00

TIMELINE	ACTION PLAN	RESPONSIBILITY
Throughout the year	Provide "train the trainer" workshops to develop staff expertise	Associate Director
Throughout the year	Work cooperatively with the State Library to provide continuing education workshops	Associate Director
Throughout the year	Support the member libraries role of training the public in select areas as determined by the Continuing Education Committee	Associate Director
By September 1996	Arrange for the reception of distance learning services	Associate Director
October 1997	Hire Continuing Education/Distance Learning Coordinator	Executive Director
October 1997 and Continuing	Train and supervise Continuing Education Coordinator to perform many of the continuing education duties previously assigned to Associate Director	Associate Director
March 1998	Develop and implement a program to provide distance learning activities	Continuing Education Coordinator and Committee
June 1998	Develop and implement a plan for a portable electronic classroom	Continuing Education Coordinator and Committee
October 1998	Develop a continuing education curriculum for paraprofessionals and explore CEU certification	Continuing Education Coordinator

GOAL 3: Technology and the Internet

Provide for resource sharing using technology and for the sharing of technological resources.

Objective 1. Make INTERNET access available through TBLC to all Member Libraries.

Objective 2. Provide network infrastructure, training, advice, and technical support to Member Libraries.

Objective 3. Coordinate local/regional access planning and support for information and database sharing.

Objective 4. Share host responsibility for statewide information resources.

Objective 5. Facilitate access to the Internet, OCLC, FILL, and FLORANET for TBLC member library staff.

Objective 6. Facilitate access through member libraries for Library users throughout the TBLC service area to the Internet, OCLC, FILL and FLORANET.

Background:

TBLC has been at the forefront of development of Internet connectivity for Florida libraries. The Internet Access for Florida's Public Libraries grant in 1993/94 enabled TBLC to explore possibilities and to implement Internet services for a pilot group of 6 libraries. This successful demonstration has been expanded to availability to all TBLC member libraries. In 1994/95 over 500 staff members from more than 50 member libraries sought accounts on the TBLC server. The program includes a strong educational element which is integrated into TBLC's continuing education role. Focus of the program is to enable library staff to use technology, to coordinate selection and/or purchase of electronic resources, to work with local, regional and state agencies in Florida in an effort to maximize electronic access at the most reasonable cost.

The **TBLC Internet Project** is planned to provide the telecommunication network, Internet host, training, technical support and regional promotion necessary to allow library staff and the public to use the Internet, OCLC, Florida's interlibrary loan system (FILL) and a collection of online government, educational, social services, humanities, medical and legal information (FLORANET).

The general methodology for the project includes: 1) providing a host computer on the Internet; 2) establishing a telecommunication network which will support local and remote toll-free dial-access; 3) providing access to the Internet, OCLC, FILL, FLORANET and other appropriate information delivery vehicles; 4) effectively training library staff and the public to use these information delivery systems.

TECHNOLOGY AND INTERNET ONGOING ACTION PLANS 1995/96 through 1999/00

TIMELINE	ACTION PLANS	RESPONSIBILITY
Throughout the year	Provide access to the Internet for Member Libraries	Internet Specialist
Throughout the year	Provide training about the Internet for Member Libraries	Associate Director
Review Annually (See below for creation of plan)	Provide a coordinated Internet service plan (including staff, fees, telecommunications, networking, training, and technical support components)	TBLC Staff, Internet Interest Group

TECHNOLOGY AND INTERNET ONGOING ACTION PLANS 1995/96 through 1999/00

TIMELINE	ACTION PLANS	RESPONSIBILITY
Throughout the year	Work with the State Library and the Florida Library Network Council (FLNC) to provide cost effective access to technology, telecommunications and electronic resources.	Executive Director
Throughout the year	Recommend content priorities to FLNC based on constituent needs	Executive Director
Throughout the year	Work with vendors, FIRN and other Florida networks to plan for the telecommunications, hardware, software and technical aspects of maintaining working electronic systems (Internet, SUNLINE)	SUNLINE Librarian
Throughout the year	Work with TBLC staff to determine the structure of access to the Internet for patrons	Internet Interest Group
Throughout the year	Collaborate with Free-Nets and other local access providers on network access structures/menu building	Internet Specialist
Throughout the year	Develop and train appropriate TBLC libraries on how to set up their own Internet nodes	SUNLINE Librarian
Throughout the year	Participate in and publicize demonstrations of "leading edge technology" within the Florida Library Community	Member Libraries
Throughout the year	Coordinate and facilitate programs to provide resources such as First Search.	Associate Director
Throughout the year	Work with an Internet Interest Group to advise TBLC and the State Library on creating useful means for providing information to librarians about Florida network resources	Associate Director
Throughout the year	Maintain and enhance access for local patrons to networked resources	Internet Interest Group and TBLC staff
Throughout the year	Structure local access to bibliographic resources to allow patrons to review local, then regional, then state resources	Internet Specialist
Throughout the year	Maintain and enhance the TBLC Internet Gopher to include Florida Freenets, SUNLINE, and access to other library cooperatives	Internet Specialist

TECHNOLOGY AND INTERNET ACTION PLANS 1995/96 - 1996/97

TIMELINE	ACTION PLANS	RESPONSIBILITY
Throughout the year	Fulfill the requirements of the statewide First Search project grant. Provide supplemental access to the limits of the original budget and work with libraries as they supplement grant funded services.	Associate Director
May 1996	Implement USENET news on TBLC's node	Internet Specialist
June 1996	Install and maintain various TBLC listservs and/or bulletin boards	Internet Specialist
November 1996	Develop a coordinated Internet service plan (including staffing, fees, telecommunications, networking, training, and technical support components)	Internet Planning Team
November 1996	Determine the structure of access to the Internet for patrons	Internet Interest Group
November 1996	Evaluate Internet menus based on input from Internet Interest Group and TBLC Staff	Internet Interest Group
November 1996	Plan for Graphical User Interface	Internet Interest Group
Throughout the year	Provide assistance with group purchase, and/or simultaneous user license agreements with vendors for member library purchase.	Executive Director, Associate Director

#55 a. -- Tampa Bay Library Consortium

141

CHART: CCLS LONG RANGE PLAN 1997 - 1999

Strategic Direction	Objectives	Year One	Timeline Year Two	Year Three
Provide high quality continuing education and training to member and associate member library staff	To offer 45-55 classes of Internet and communications technologies related training classes to member and associate member library staffs	Internet and ACLIN training	communications training to meet as yet undetermined needs	communications training to meet as yet undetermined needs
	To offer 10-15 programs on a variety of library and management topics to member and associate member library staffs	series of 8 classes on supervision; other classes to be determined	classes to be determined by assessment of needs	classes to be determined by assessment of needs
	To hold a "technology fair" in cooperation with other regional library systems with exhibits, information sessions and demonstrations, covering technology of all types including the Internet, local area networking, CD ROM and home information technology	technology fair -- winter 97	programs to be identified by future needs	programs to be identified by future needs
	To hold a "Children's Institute" in cooperation with other regional library systems providing specialized training to update school/public librarians and media specialists on current needs of youth which can/may be addressed with improved services, facilities, and awareness. Academic or recertification credit will be available if possible	Children's Services Institute -- summer 97	programs to be identified by future needs	programs to be identified by future needs

	To explore distance learning opportunities for member libraries and downlink one teleconference of interest to members	offer at least 1 teleconference; publicize additional events	continue to identify and offer distance learning events	continue to identify and offer distance learning events
	To take a leadership role in development of statewide plan for continuing education	assist in development of needs assessment, telecommunications, and projects related to statewide plan	assist in updating and evaluation of statewide plan if necessary	assist in updating and evaluation of statewide plan if necessary
Facilitate access to information and information delivery; encourage resource sharing	To prepare and distribute four issues of the publication "Midnight at the Internet Cafe"	produce four issues of "Midnight" on varying topics	assess needs for continuation and produce if need exists	assess needs for continuation and produce if need exists
	To provide courier service to members and associates and provide links to other system couriers to establish as large a network as possible of libraries throughout the state	provide courier service, assess additional needs, evaluate performance	provide courier service, assess additional needs, evaluate performance	provide courier service, assess additional needs, evaluate performance
	To develop follow-up proposals for statewide courier development	follow-up proposal completed and implemented	review and modify where appropriate	review and modify where appropriate
	To initiate WEBSTER project	initiate WEBSTER project	assess project, expand or modify as needed	assess project, expand or modify as needed
	To ensure that CCLS libraries maintain priority ILL status when borrowing from UC Boulder libraries by providing funding for clerical support in Norlin ILL department	provide funding to maintain CCLS priority status at UC Boulder	assess need for continuation; continue or modify as needed	assess need for continuation; continue or modify as needed

Provide process management and technical assistance	To provide assistance to member and associate members in developing a planning process and facilitating planning meetings	assist libraries in planning as needed	assist libraries in planning as needed	assist libraries in planning as needed	assist libraries in planning as needed
	To conduct one or two planning or meeting facilitation workshops for other regional systems in Colorado	conduct workshops if requested and as time allows	conduct workshops if requested and as time allows	conduct workshops if requested and as time allows	conduct workshops if requested and as time allows
	To provide meeting facilitation to members and associate members	provide meeting facilitation as requested	provide meeting facilitation as requested	provide meeting facilitation as requested	provide meeting facilitation as requested
	To provide consulting assistance to member libraries in areas that are within the scope of staff expertise e.g. space planning, desktop publishing	provide consulting assistance as requested	provide consulting assistance as requested	provide consulting assistance as requested	provide consulting assistance as requested
Provide business support to CCLS libraries	To maintain trust accounts for CCLS libraries	maintain trust accounts	continue accounts as needed	continue accounts as needed	continue accounts as needed
	To submit a proposal to the Colorado Library Resource Sharing Board for a statewide pilot test of Gale electronic publications. If accepted, to conduct and maintain the test in cooperation with the Consortium on database networking. The expected outcome is a negotiated statewide discount for libraries	draft proposal for pilot test	evaluate test; continue if desirable	evaluate test; continue if desirable	evaluate test; continue if desirable

Provide professional advocacy and leadership				
	To advocate statewide funding for libraries by providing information to and making contacts with library trustees, school boards and administrators, teacher groups and others who will influence the adoption of library funding	Director, with CCLS Board, will advocate statewide funding for libraries by providing information to and making contacts with library trustees, school boards and administrators, teacher groups and others who will influence the adoption of library funding	Director will take advocacy role in library funding issues	Director will take advocacy role in library funding issues
	To facilitate and participate in the work of the "crisis in school libraries" committee. Work with a subgroup of the committee and professional organizations to develop a presence at the school administrators annual conference	Director will facilitate and participate in the work of the "crisis in the school libraries committee". Work with a subgroup of the committee and professional organizations to develop a presence at the school admin annual conference	Director will assess success of committee and continue if needed	Director will assess success of committee and continue if needed
	To write and distribute 10 issues of the CCLS newsletter NEXUS, adding an electronic format by end of year	publish Nexus -- 10 issues, including electronic format by end of year	evaluate need, frequency, and format; continue or change as necessary	evaluate need, frequency, and format; continue or change as necessary

To participate actively in system directors' meetings and work to influence the group to adopt more standardized procedures in accounting and auditing, including the development of a standard chart of accounts for systems	Director will actively participate in system directors' meetings and work to influence the group to adopt more standardized procedures in accounts and auditing, including the development of a standard chart of accounts for systems	Director will continue to work with system directors' to accomplish common objectives and advocate standardization	Director will continue to work with system directors' to accomplish common objectives and advocate standardization
To participate in task forces, interest groups, and other meetings and conferences addressing statewide and member library issues and cooperative projects	Director and Assistant Director will participate in task forces, interest groups, and other meetings and conferences addressing statewide and member library issues and cooperative projects	Director and Assistant Director will participate in task forces, interest groups, and other meetings and conferences addressing statewide and member library issues and cooperative projects.	Director and Assistant Director will participate in task forces, interest groups, and other meetings and conferences addressing statewide and member library issues and cooperative projects.

To be a member of and actively participate in state, regional and national professional associations	Director will carry out duties as member of Executive Committee of ALA's Interlibrary Cooperation and Networking Section and member of CLA's legislative committee. Assistant Director will carry out duties as President of MPLA and maintain membership in CLA.	Assistant Director will carry out duties as Past President of MPLA and maintain membership in CLA	Director and Assistant Director will continue active professional involvement

#8 -- Central Colorado Library System

147

CHAPTER 8

EVALUATION

EVALUATION

Evaluation in the context of library cooperative and system strategic planning almost always involves two components: (1) evaluation of how well the plan itself worked in moving the organization towards the desired results and (2) evaluation of the performance of the organization during the period of the plan. These evaluations typically examine the recent accomplishments of the organization in terms of some performance measures or benchmarks. In order to tie this evaluation process back into the strategic planning process, it is helpful to build as many of these benchmarks as possible into the planning document. To maximize effectiveness and consistency, the planning process should incorporate a cycle for evaluation so that the timing is coordinated with the next planning cycle.

Any data that can help the cooperative or system to understand its present capabilities are helpful in the evaluative component. These might include life cycles of products/services, employee productivity, facilities and management capability. Effectively performed, the evaluation process can provide a number of benefits:

- an indication of the organization's capacity to move in the desired strategic directions,
- objective look at the strategies in place and progress being made by the organization,
- validation of the cooperative's successes in quantifiable measures,
- early data on emerging "next wave" of strategies to build upon developing trends and organizational strengths.

Among the submitted plans, information on evaluation strategies was scarce. As was noted in Chapter 2, however, organizational approaches to the planning process are often articulated in separate documents. Since evaluation is clearly a part of the overall process, it is likely that some organizations do not include evaluation in their strategic plans but define the process separately. Another piece to this element is the way in which the plan's objectives are formulated. To the extent they are measurable and have an associated deadline, an obvious met/unmet evaluation may apply. It should be noted, however, that in plans that are taking a truly strategic look at futures, objectives of this type can be problematic.

In reviewing those plans that did provide information on the topic, responsibility for the evaluation often included both member and staff components. Measurement criteria and methodologies were outlined in several and often included annual surveys. In at least one, a chronicle of accomplishments tied to the last plan was included, offering an evaluation as preface to the current planning effort.

EVALUATION BENCHMARKS

This plan creates a framework within which the Region will operate for the next five years. At the beginning of each year specific objectives, defined as measurable, specific results, will be established within each area of the plan. During the year programs will be implemented by the Region V committees and Staff. At the end of each year progress within the plan will be measured against those desired outcomes. The Board and Staff will seek to understand how and why objectives were or were not achieved. Based on that analysis, and a re-examination of the environment in which the Region operates, the plan itself will be updated and new objectives will be established for the upcoming year.

In order to measure overall success, certain evaluation benchmarks have been considered. Evaluation benchmarks answer the questions, "How do we measure a success?" and "How will we know things are working?" While specific objectives in these areas will be established annually, the following constitute overall indicators of success within the scope of the plan:

- Greater member participation in Region V services. Most members use at least one Region V service each year.
- All members are aware of Region V services. Programs are highly visible and recognized among members.
- Closer alignment between member expectations and Region V services.
- Continuing satisfaction with strong programs, such as Comet Delivery, Continuing Education and Children's Book Evaluation.
- Fewer problems with Region V services.
- The plan is used as a guideline for decision making in Region V.

Since many of these indicators refer to member awareness and satisfaction, periodic surveys of the membership will be taken to determine their awareness of Region V services and their level of satisfaction with those services. These general surveys will supplement targeted surveys for specific program areas.

#10 a. -- Central Jersey Regional Library Cooperative

EVALUATION OF SYSTEM SERVICES

The Southeast Library System will monitor and evaluate its services, programs, and staff throughout the year. The primary service evaluation tool is the annual survey, which is distributed through the System newsletter. Each individual workshop will include an evaluation form for participants to complete. System contracting centers will submit quarterly and annual reports for review by the System Board of Directors. Annual performance evaluations of System staff will take place. System committees will monitor and evaluate activities for which each is responsible. The System Strategic Plan will be used as a basis for measurable service and programming objectives. Results of all the evaluations will enhance the ability of the Southeast Library System to assess and address the needs of System members.

The Strategic Plan includes target dates for the completion of specific objectives, thereby making assessment easier.

#51 -- Southeast Nebraska Library System

Evaluation and Review Process

A Review Committee will be established to evaluate the Strategic Plan. Four to six directors of member libraries will serve on the Committee.

Six months after the Strategic Plan has been initiated, the Review Committee will convene for a preliminary evaluation. The Committee will seek input from the Executive Director, Executive Committee and chairs of standing committees. The initial review will look at:

   a) the accuracy of the Needs Assessment.
   b) the appropriateness of the Mission Statement and Goals.
   c) the effectiveness of the Action Plan.
   d) the viability of the Financial Plan.

The Committee will submit its findings to the Executive Committee. This report could include suggestions for monitoring or revising aspects of the Plan. The Committee will also prepare a survey on the Strategic Plan to be distributed to members. The survey will address issues identified in the initial review and will update information derived from earlier surveys used in establishing the Strategic Plan. The survey should be distributed within three months of the Committee's initial meeting.

A comprehensive evaluation will be made at the end of each year of the Plan. At the conclusion of the first year, the Review Committee will analyze the survey results and re-evaluate the mid-year review findings and decisions. The Purpose and Overview of the Plan will be examined. An evaluation of the Review Process will be made. Recommendations for revising and monitoring aspects of the Plan will be submitted to the Executive Committee. These recommendations, and any actions taken, will become the basis for the next mid-year review.

An annual survey will be included in the Evaluation and Review Process.

#30 -- Minuteman Library Network

Maintenance of the Long-Range Plan

All plans need to be evaluated on a regular basis. This plan will enable the MOLO organization to be responsive to rapid changes in library operations, funding opportunities, and new programs as long as it stays true to MOLO's mission statement.

1. The MOLO Executive Director and staff will work out programs in each of the areas identified within the fiscal year, report on progress made in each of these roles and provide feedback for the annual review of the Long-Range Plan.
2. After the first year in effect, the MOLO Board will form a Long-Range Plan Review Committee from the Membership Council to review the priorities in the Fall of each year and make recommendations, if needed, for any changes. Input will be sought from Interest Group Chairs, and other interested parties in compiling recommendations. Such recommendations could be modifications in roles priorities, additions of new programs/services to pursue, or identify those programs/services to sunset with a time line for removal. This review provides for a flexible, yet directed, long-range plan for the MOLO organization.

#31 -- MOLO Regional Library System

North Country Reference and Research Resources Council
Plan of Development 1996 - 2000

Goals/Objectives/Activities/Tasks	Target Year/Years					Target Completion Date	Position/Committee Responsible
	1996	1997	1998	1999	2000		
VIII. COUNCIL GOAL FOR EVALUATION: NCR'S Council activities will be evaluated on a regular basis.							
1. Membership: Major Council activities and programs will be evaluated biannually by the membership through written survey instruments.		X		X		Biannually	Executive Director/NC3R'S Staff/Board
2. Annual review and update of the NC3R'S Council's Plan of Service:	X	X	X	X	X	On-going	Executive Director/Committees/Board
a. The Council's Plan of Development will be reviewed annually, with the Executive Director reporting to the Board of Trustees concerning the status of objectives, activities, and tasks scheduled for the year.							

#38 -- North Country Reference & Research Resources Council

154

Accomplishments

Since its last plan was adopted in 1993, the SEFLIN Board, members, and staff have worked diligently through the joint use of technology to achieve many of the plan's goals and objectives. A review of significant SEFLIN accomplishments from 1993 - 1996 provides tangible proof of the value of SEFLIN and its impact on the South Florida library environment. Among the most significant accomplishments are:

- The design, implementation and continued operation of the SEFLIN Free-Net in Dade, Broward and Palm Beach Counties and the phenomenal public response resulting in 40,000 registrants accessing the system over 2 million times in less than two years;

- Successful advocacy efforts resulting in state funds to support multitype library cooperation;

- Joint use of technology for group subscriptions to CD-ROM databases;

- Strengthened SEFLIN's financial resources through the addition of state and local grants, a federal NTIA grant and targeting reserve funds;

- Delivery of an ever-expanding array of continuing education programs attracting more than 500 members per year;

- A firm member commitment to SEFLIN as an organization that can design and facilitate cutting edge programs and encourage transformation and innovation in member libraries;

- Free-Net training resulting in over 8,000 members of the public trained each year;

- The addition of new members representing school and special libraries and additional geographic coverage;

- Expanded and enhanced courier service;

- The SEFLIN library card program;

- Participation in the statewide First Search project for joint use of technology for sharing online information resources;

- A pilot project for an electronic reference desk;

- A comprehensive catalog of government documents held in member libraries;

- Maintenance of a high-quality serials union list; and

- An expanded staff with a broader range of expertise and skills that benefit member libraries and library customers.

#50 a. -- Southeast Florida Library Information Network, Inc.

CHAPTER 9

FORMAT, DESIGN
&
MARKETING

FORMAT, DESIGN & MARKETING

This book is an effort to compile different parts of strategic plans in each chapter as a basis for comparison and review. The original formatting of the documents could be reproduced only to a limited degree; therefore, it is important to see the graphics and formatting features of the samples in this chapter. Throughout this book we have emphasized that the strategic plans of different organizations have been shaped by the environment, the target audience and the purpose of the plan. The plans submitted varied in format from sophisticated to simple, from easy to skim to dense and from quick copy to professional printing quality. The planning and printing budgets of the organizations obviously spanned a wide range.

BENEFITS
Strategic plans are often used as marketing and fundraising tools, as well as, internal organizational documents. Even at the most basic level, the strategic plan of a library cooperative can be a powerful communication tool with the membership and stakeholders. The success of the implementation of the strategic plan depends on the understanding of the members, staff, Board and others. The format and design of the strategic plan can be very effective even with a limited budget.

FORMAT
Photographs and professional layouts can make a dramatic statement, such as the examples from the California State Library and Council of Wisconsin Libraries. Several examples in this chapter show the use of the organization's logo for the cover and as design elements throughout the document. There are examples of a summary or brochure format which were used in addition to the more formal document. The Cleveland Area Metropolitan Library System submitted a version from their newsletter. These summary formats could be posted on a bulletin board for a constant reminder of the organization's direction.

Graphics and photographs are effective; but, the goal is to make the document as easy to read as possible. The more bullets and white space in the document, the easier it is to use. Simple techniques like two columns, boxes, shading, bold lettering and reverse type can make a difference as the samples in this section demonstrate.

WEB SITES
The Web offers a new format and distribution tool for strategic plans. More and more library cooperatives have Web sites but only a few submitted samples which included their strategic plans. The Web sites included plans which ranged from simple DOS text to graphical formats and charts. The world of Web sites is a rapidly changing environment which should quickly include a large number of plans.

FORMAT & DESIGN EXAMPLES

The following examples do not have page numbers added to the pages which are reproduced from the original documents. The reference numbers and organizations are listed below in the order which the documents are included in this publication.

 # 6. California State Library

 # 15. Council Of Wisconsin Libraries, Inc. (COWL

 # 43. PALINET

 # 50. Southeast Florida Library Information Network, Inc. (SEFLIN),
       b. LRSP Summary

 # 12. Cleveland Area Metropolitan Library System (CAMLS)

 # 51. Southeast Nebraska Library System

 # 2. Bergen County Cooperative Library System (BCCLS

 # 18. Georgia Department of Education, Public Library Services

 # 47. South Carolina State Library

 # 21. Indiana State Library

WEB ACCESS - SAMPLE SITES

http://www.colosys.net/swrlss/plan.htm
    # 54 - Southwest Regional Library Service System (SWRLSS)

http://lrs.stcloud.msus.edu/cmle/plan.html
    # 11 - Central Minnesota Libraries Exchange (CMLE)

http://www.seflin.org/seflink/
    # 50 - Southeast Florida Library Information Network, Inc. (SEFLIN)

http://www.amigos.org/plan2000.html
    # 1 - AMIGOS

Strategic Plan
1995 - 2000

INTO THE HIGHLANDS OF THE MIND LET ME GO

California State Library, Sacramento

1850 - 2000 A.D.

150 Years

California State Library
Sacramento, California

Strategic Plan 1995 - 2000

California State Library
Sacramento, California

Our Vision

**The California State Library
will be the most dynamic
state library in the nation
and will be recognized as such.**

Strategy I   *Provide Quality Information Services*

We intend to move further in the direction of a library driven by customer demand and the customer's need to cope with information overload. Such a change is necessary to provide quality information services to those in state government who may not have enough time to know what information is available, let alone learn how to obtain it. In all its efforts, the State Library will assist the people of California in gaining electronic access to the information resources of state government.

(California State Capitol, 1995)

STRATEGY 1.1   REASSESS AND REALIGN LIBRARY SERVICES

ISSUE   *A dynamic economic, political and technological environment demands that we stay in touch with and position ourselves to respond to the rapidly changing information needs of both state government and the public.*

GOALS   • Reassess customer needs for timeliness, convenience, and delivery methods for information services.

• Realign library services as suggested by changing needs of customers.

STRATEGY 1.2   MAXIMIZE TECHNOLOGY PARTNERSHIPS

ISSUE   *Rapidly changing technology, coupled with increasing costs and continuing competition for scarce public and private resources, requires that we optimize existing inter-agency, community, and library partnerships and actively pursue new partnerships in order to maximize our investments in technology and to develop and achieve our shared objectives.*

GOALS   • Help make state and local agency information available on the Internet.

• Promote effective public and state agency use of the resources of the Internet by working with libraries and agency partners to identify and/or develop training and navigational tools.

Council of Wisconsin Libraries
Strategic Plan

For Information Access & Resource Sharing: Year 2000

PREFACE

The Council of Wisconsin Libraries (COWL) is a not-for-profit corporation founded in 1972 with a mission of facilitating library resource sharing within the state; that is, to concentrate on research, design and development of new and innovative programs of resource sharing that will assist libraries in making information resources available to all library users in Wisconsin. COWL is an organization composed of representatives of all sizes and types of libraries who serve as the governing board for COWL-sponsored service programs (WILS); who study and discuss issues of concern and opportunity for libraries; and who make decisions on new or enhanced programs for the Wisconsin library community.

COWL must position itself, and the libraries it represents, to meet the immediate challenges of the changing information environment and be prepared to address the needs and opportunities of the foreseeable future. Thus COWL has initiated a strategic planning process to review the definition of resource sharing within the current environment; to identify new directions in library cooperation that would better meet future needs of libraries; and to assess the continued viability of its organizational goals and service programs.

the cost effectiveness of cataloging for individual libraries, but more importantly, from the collective perspective, created a national database for interlibrary loan and formed a foundation from which libraries have built their online catalogs. These online catalogs now become the foundation for a virtual statewide database necessary for achieving the resource sharing vision.

Resource sharing of reference and information services in a virtual Wisconsin library must involve selection of electronic resources, cooperative purchase and licensing for statewide access, training for library staff in the use of such tools and a communication system for librarians and library users to access the human expertise within Wisconsin's libraries to facilitate the use of electronic tools.

Many Wisconsin libraries are already sharing electronic resources through group licensing of electronic indexes, use of the Internet for accessing electronic resources, and use of services such as OCLC's FirstSearch. Individual libraries must determine the electronic resources necessary for their users; however, it is clear from the experiences of other states, such as Minnesota and Ohio, that the collective buying power of a group of libraries will achieve a better price for electronic products. COWL has done cooperative purchasing for libraries for nearly ten years, and as an independent corporation has the organizational flexibility to extend this service to include electronic indexes and electronic full text.

Setting Goals

Traditional interlibrary loan is well developed and coordinated in Wisconsin. The State Library Agency and its public library systems provide direct service and coordinate interloan for public and school libraries; COWL, through WILS, provides direct service and serves as the access point to the state's academic library resources. A virtual database will improve access to the State's library resources but without equivalent improvements in lending processes and turn-around-time for delivery of materials and information to patrons, as well as resolution of the lending equity issue, the database will not reach its full potential.

New technologies, particularly the Internet and the emergence of community networks, have caused a questioning in some arenas as to the long term value of libraries in an electronic world. The fact is that libraries are frequently the leaders in applying new technologies to the information business. Community networks are developing in Wisconsin; two are already operational, and libraries have been leaders in using the Internet. Sharing of experiences and expertise with other community network planners to enhance the quality of service, and leadership in linking of these networks, must be part of the resource sharing

vision. This is an area where COWL's leadership, through the WILS New Technologies Information Service, in monitoring national developments, sharing information through *New Tech News*, consulting with local groups, training users, and serving as a clearinghouse of relevant technological materials and of current activities, will be critical.

Another important area is Distance Education. Distance Education is a statewide initiative which offers opportunities while posing technological and service challenges for Wisconsin libraries. It offers positive options for staff development and training; it poses new challenges for libraries in providing services to distance learners. Initiated and inspired by the work of the COWL ad hoc Distance Learning Planning Committee of the early nineties, WILS has taken a leadership role in delivering training programs via interactive video. This application improves accessibility to educational programs while saving member libraries staff time and travel expense. The challenge that remains is assisting libraries in providing intellectual access, bibliographic instruction, reference service and document delivery to distance education teachers and learners.

Finally, the vision of resource sharing cannot be achieved with the current level of funding for libraries. In order to increase library funding it will be necessary to increase the visibility, and improve the image, of libraries in the eyes of the funding agencies. As an organization of libraries, COWL is structured to take on this challenge through its representatives of the library community.

INTRODUCTION

PALINET's current strategic plan was developed in 1990, and issued in 1991 January. While this plan has served the network well, the changes that have occurred in libraries over the last few years argued strongly for a review and revision of the plan.

The Board of Trustees undertook the task of revising and updating the plan in 1994 and early 1995. This work led the Board to the conclusion that the major goals of the original plan—providing leadership, supporting OCLC services, influencing change, developing partnerships, providing member staff support and assisting in forging linkages—did not require radical change. What had changed during the preceding five years, and what will continue to change at an even more rapid pace in the future, is the context in which libraries and PALINET operate.

The revised and updated PALINET Long-Range Strategic Plan that the Board approved and adopted on 1995 May 31 is presented beginning with the vision statement. Major paradigm shifts that PALINET believes will affect libraries, and thus PALINET as an operating entity, are summarized following this introduction. Initial priorities for implementation of strategies are presented in the appendix.

Vision Statement

PALINET leads libraries in shaping tomorrow for themselves and their customers. PALINET is entrepreneurial, member supportive and a key source of technical expertise.

Vision is a futuristic picture of the organization. This vision statement demands that PALINET exercise leadership in helping libraries to shape their tomorrows, not be shaped by them. It indicates that PALINET must be an agile organization, able to capitalize on opportunities as they arise and to maintain the technical expertise necessary to do so, while maintaining a strong orientation to ongoing service and support of its members and customers.

PALINET
Libraries shaping tomorrow™

New Horizons for
SEFLIN 2000

**Long Range
Strategic Plan
1996-2000**

June 1996

OUR MISSION

SEFLIN, a non-profit membership organization of Southeast Florida libraries, believes that libraries can make a difference in people's lives. Our mission is to work cooperatively with our members and the community to promote the collection and sharing of library resources, to facilitate training, to increase public awareness, to provide leadership, to encourage the joint use of technology and to support activities that enhance an individual library's ability to meet the informational, educational and cultural needs of its primary users and Southeast Florida residents.

OUR VISION

SEFLIN member libraries are committed to working cooperatively and using the SEFLIN organization to assist libraries in meeting their individual service missions.

SEFLIN will position SEFLIN libraries as major leaders in the information structure of Southeast Florida by working cooperatively with libraries, educational institutions, information agencies, area businesses and government agencies. SEFLIN will enable libraries to transcend political boundaries and empower people to receive the information they need when they need it. SEFLIN libraries will affirm the social value of libraries as key contributors to the community's social and economic well-being and quality of life. SEFLIN libraries will facilitate the joint use of technology to provide the residents of Southeast Florida with links to local, state, regional, and global information resources.

To accomplish this, SEFLIN will remain a cooperative membership organization that provides an organizational structure that facilitates:

- the delivery of a wide range of services to meet specific regional needs;

- sharing of traditional library materials and electronic information resources;

- continuing education and training of library staff to accommodate changing roles and technological advances;

- leadership and advocacy for the advancement of libraries;

- experimentation and innovation with new technologies designed to improve the delivery of library service.

STRATEGIC ISSUES

During the planning session, the SEFLIN Board of Directors and Committees identified a number of strategic issues that will affect libraries and the way in which library services are delivered in the next few years. These issues will also have an impact on SEFLIN's services and products.

■ A CHANGING INFORMATION ENVIRONMENT

The information environment is rapidly changing with the development of community networks, commercial information services, world wide web resources, and other new technological innovations that make it easier to locate and obtain information. We are moving away from a centralized, controlled information environment to a decentralized model where a wide variety of organizations and individuals may contribute to the development and access of information tools. SEFLIN can become an active participant in shaping the Southeast Florida information environment by allocating resources and forging partnerships with other information and telecommunication providers and developing relationships that will meet the needs of its members and the customers they serve.

■ NEW LIBRARY PRACTICES

Libraries are considering new ways to handle different library practices. Out-sourcing of technical services, new ways to deliver training and continuing education, and increased use of technology will transform the traditional ways in which libraries do business. SEFLIN can help its members in making these transitions and explore options for delivering these services on a regional basis.

■ DELIVERY OF SERVICES

Information is becoming increasingly available in electronic formats. The availability of full-text periodical databases and commercial document delivery services is requiring many libraries to rethink their collection development practices. The role of libraries as depositories of printed information may become too costly to continue. SEFLIN will explore options for group licensing of information products and cooperative collection development in an electronic environment.

■ CONTROLLING COSTS

Pressure to control library expenditures at the local level continues to increase each year. SEFLIN can play an important role in assisting its members in negotiating preferential rates for telecommunications and group purchase contracts of print and electronic information products. Grants will continue to be an important resource for funding research and development.

■ LEADERSHIP

The SEFLIN Committee structure can be strengthened to ensure that members have the skills needed to engage in productive problem solving, project management, and decision-making. SEFLIN will continuously examine more effective ways to deliver service.

6

1994-1997

Goal 1. Maximize access to resources in and beyond members' collections

Desired Results:
75% of members have Internet access.

100% of members have holdings on the Union List.

A CAMLS workstation is defined and deployed.

Goal 2. Develop the financial resources of CAMLS to meet program needs

Desired Results:
CAMLS membership totals 85.

CAMLS financial reserves are increased by $10,000.

CAMLS CE program is positioned to be self-supporting.

CAMLS STRATEGIC PLAN

Goal 5. Address critical community issues for the benefit of the Greater Cleveland area

Desired Results:
CAMLS libraries are recognized as leaders in service to diverse populations.

CAMLS libraries are recognized as full partners in community actions to enhance the economic and educational environment.

Goal 3. Establish the foundation for an income-generating, cutting-edge Continuing Education program

Desired Results:
Continuing Education is provided in a multi-year sequence of programs organized around member-driven themes.

Goal 4. Provide expert matchmaking to enhance members' efficiency and effectiveness

Desired Results:
CAMLS facilitates multi-library partnerships and serves as an information clearinghouse in selected areas.

CAMLS
Cleveland Area Metropolitan Library System

OUR PURPOSE

CAMLS will help the libraries of the Greater Cleveland area achieve such an effective and efficient sharing of information, resources, and expertise that they become the very best they can be and the area itself flourishes.

OUR VISION

CAMLS is a membership consortium of public, academic, special, and school libraries in the Greater Cleveland area. We have worked together since 1977 to enhance the information richness of the area and to bring high quality services to citizens. Historically, we have led the way as libraries faced the challenges of the times. As we enter the new century, the environment is characterized by uncertainty, fast-paced technological change, and increasing budgetary concerns, making our collaboration all the more essential.

CAMLS remains the vital link between all types of libraries in the Greater Cleveland area. It enables them to achieve their own goals of excellence and to be more than they could be alone. CAMLS libraries maximize their potential through collaboration, cooperation, and partnership with each other, other networks, and other organizations.

Together, CAMLS members harness the power of information technology and the expertise of information professionals for the improvement and benefit of the entire community. Through CAMLS, we achieve our dream of providing seamless access to information for library staff and those they serve. CAMLS members are models of innovation, creativity, and excellence, and together lead the nation in providing equitable services and broad access to information.

CAMLS brings ideas, resources, and people together to address the critical community issues of the times. We encourage an environment that fosters change, leadership, and empowerment of both library staff and citizens. CAMLS connects members with each other and with outside organizations and programs, serving as a broker and referral source to help libraries meet their needs. The high quality staff in the CAMLS office serve as a clearinghouse for information when librarians need assistance. They develop and coordinate cooperative ventures, and help libraries plan and find funding for special projects that will benefit the library community and those they serve.

Through CAMLS, a wide array of affordable services is available, and new services are developed to meet changing needs. CAMLS is seen as the major provider of leading-edge continuing education by the Greater Cleveland library community. We anticipate members' needs and provide top quality educational experiences for leadership, technological change, and systematic professional development.

CAMLS programs, services, and networking opportunities are indispensable to the area's libraries and librarians. Thanks to CAMLS, Greater Cleveland is assured that its libraries will continue to bring our collective resources and expertise to bear on the opportunities and challenges of the future.

Approved by the CAMLS Board of Trustees, 12/16/93   CAMLS News, Vol. 16, No. 1

5

Southeast Library System Strategic Plan   1995-1997

Vision Statement

The Southeast Library System envisions a world where libraries and individuals have direct and equal access to the diverse resources needed for education, work and leisure. Technological developments will continue to challenge us to help libraries keep pace with the changing role of our profession.

Mission Statement

The Southeast Library System works proactively with library personnel and with other agencies to help them meet the diverse informational needs of their patrons. Innovative, interdependent and seamless approaches will be used to provide services.

Function Statement

The Southeast Library System is one of six regional library systems in Nebraska. Our state and federal funding enables our role as a provider of library development services to all kinds of libraries in our 15 county region.

Service roles have been defined as Technology Development, Resource Sharing / Reference, Continuing Education, and Library Support.

Purpose of the Plan

The Strategic Plan will outline goals and strategies for the two year period July 1995 through June 1997.

Goals

1. Continue to offer support for resource sharing activities while pursuing interdependence, seamless access, seamless delivery, and equity of access.

2. Improve individual libraries' ability to offer reference and information services to patrons, including the use of print, electronic and online sources.

3. Work with libraries in the System to enhance their ability to implement technology and electronic resources in their operations.

4. Offer quality continuing education opportunities for diverse needs and audiences, especially within primary and secondary System service roles.

5. Offer consultation services within the primary and secondary System service roles; facilitate consultation among peers.

6. Work with library development leaders for reciprocal support, feedback, and cooperation.

7. Use resources as available for special projects, such as the cooperative video license.

Goals and Strategies (with target dates)

> **Goal 1**
> Continue to offer support for resource sharing activities while pursuing interdependence, seamless access, seamless delivery, and equity of access.

- Shift 70% of sites currently dependent on ILL resource center service toward more independent ILL. (June 1997)

- Maintain existing resource center contracts during development and transition toward new goals.

- Work towards a broader means of electronic access to Nebraska libraries' holdings, either through a union catalog or through other innovative methods. (August 1995)

- Examine and choose the most efficient and cost effective delivery system for interlibrary loan in southeast Nebraska. (August 1995)

- Develop educational requirements for the use of the System resource centers. (July 1995)

- Incorporate policies of responsibility in conjunction with use of the ILL/Reference services; include Rule Statements and guidelines devised by the System and enforced by the Center. (July 1995)

- Create an ILL training video for System members' use. (July 1996)

- Continue to analyze and implement charges for use of System resource centers.

- Announce the fade of the 800# for resource centers; discontinue 800#s. (August 96/ December 96)

Goal 2
Improve individual libraries' ability to offer reference and information services to patrons, including the use of print, electronic and online sources.

- Work with the Nebraska Library Commission to offer subsidized access to databases such as OCLC's FirstSearch. (December 1995)

- Offer Internet training and access assistance. (ongoing)

- Offer reference materials training, using the STAR Reference Manual (Fall 1995 / Spring 1996 / Fall 1997)

- Offer reference interview training in conjunction with STAR Manual workshops. (Fall 1995 / Spring 1996 / Fall 1997)

Goal 3
Work with libraries in the System to enhance their ability to implement technology and electronic resources in their operations.

- Offer technology showcase workshop which highlights emerging technologies. (Fall 1995)

- Assist libraries in obtaining financial assistance for hardware purchases. (ongoing)

- Work with the Nebraska Library Commission and Nebrask@Interactive to provide uniform and affordable Internet access. (January 1996)

- Assist libraries in developing Internet connections, including SLIP/PPP connections. (ongoing)

- Continue to provide a site license for Alliance Plus (the Follett bibliographic CD for data conversion). (ongoing)

- Employ a part time technology consultant to make onsite visits to libraries who have questions and concerns in technology development and implementation. (July 1995)

Goal 4
Offer quality continuing education opportunities for diverse needs and audiences, especially within primary and secondary System service roles.

- In addition to continuing education opportunities highlighted in previous goal statements, offer training in multi-cultural programming, children's and young adult programming, community analysis, people skills, trustee training, and basic library skills. (ongoing)

- Facilitate interest group discussions and meetings, such as the Follett user group meetings. (ongoing)

- Continue to poll membership for continuing education needs. (ongoing)

- Work with other regional library systems to deliver continuing education programs. (ongoing)

Goal 5
Offer consultation services within the primary and secondary System service roles; facilitate consultation among peers.

- Provide WATS line to the System office for member use.

- Publish a newsletter 10 times per year, to include information on library development.

- Provide incentives for mentoring among librarians, including grants to participants. (August 1996)

- Continue to provide support for Children's Services through the provision of a Juvenile Resource Center.

- Review current Children's Services; make appropriate recommendations. (April 1996)

- Continue to provide professional journals for routing to member libraries. Increase or change titles as needed for emerging interests. (ongoing)

- Purchase a System car for Administrator travel. (July 1995)

Goal 6
Work with library development leaders for reciprocal support, feedback, and cooperation.

- System Administrator will attend meetings with peers and with Nebraska Library Commission staff. (ongoing)

- System Administrator will participate in broad planning initiatives in Nebraska, keeping Southeast Library System goals and objectives in the forefront of discussions. (ongoing)

Plan of Service

BERGEN COUNTY

BCCLS

COOPERATIVE
LIBRARY SYSTEM

I. Reference and Technology

1. Strengthen reference resources available to Bergen County residents
   A. Hire a consultant to develop recommendations for enhancing reference service to the public
   B. Encourage continued cooperation between member libraries in providing reference services

2. Increase flexibility of DRA workstations with continued implementation of PC based, rather than dumb terminal, software

3. Improve the user friendliness of the OPAC interface
   A. Use focus groups to work with BCCLS staff members on PC and non-PC products

4. Work toward preferential telecommunications rates for libraries and patrons communicating with libraries
   A. Request discounts from the telecommunications industry
   B. Request support from public officials, if necessary

5. Develop the role of the Internet as a major vehicle for library service
   A. Investigate school resources for local Internet developments
   B. Address non-bibliographic files, such as community information files

6. Implement CD-ROM as part of the BCCLS profile
   A. Catalog CD-ROM circulating and reference items
   B. Enhance resources for CD-ROM use in the library

II. Communication, Cooperation and In-Service Training

1. Establish a staff development committee with a two-year charge to determine the viability of said committee to:
   A. Continue staff exchanges for various departments on a regular basis
   B. Arrange professional development programs focusing on topics of interest
   C. Provide guidelines for writing manuals covering basic library operations
   D. Encourage visits to libraries beyond Bergen County for examples of effective service and programs
   E. Sponsor one or two Publisher's Days each year: CD-ROM, children, reference, vocational guidance, etc.

LONG-RANGE PROGRAM
FOR GEORGIA PUBLIC LIBRARIES
1995 - 1999

Georgia Department of Education
Public Library Services
August, 1995

South Carolina State Library

Strategic Plan

1996 - 1999

SOUTH CAROLINA
STATE
LIBRARY

1996

SOUTH CAROLINA STATE LIBRARY
STRATEGIC PLAN
1996-1999

I. MISSION

The South Carolina State Library's mission is to improve library services throughout the state and to ensure all citizens access to libraries and information resources adequate to meet their needs. The State Library supports libraries in meeting the informational, educational, cultural, and recreational needs of the people of South Carolina.

II. VALUES

A. QUALITY

The South Carolina State Library endeavors to provide services of the highest quality.

B. KNOWLEDGE

The South Carolina State Library believes that a well-trained and knowledgeable staff is its greatest asset.

C. FREEDOM OF INFORMATION

The South Carolina State Library believes freedom of expression is a fundamental right of a democratic society and supports the Library Bill of Rights and the Freedom to Read Statement.

D. ACCESS TO INFORMATION

The South Carolina State Library believes that all citizens regardless of their location or means should have access to library and information services.

E. EQUITABLE TREATMENT

The South Carolina State Library provides services to its customers in a fair and unbiased manner.

III. VISION

The South Carolina State Library is a major leader in the planning and implementation of effective informational and library services for the people of South Carolina. It is a vital component of the State's information infrastructure.

IV. ROLE STATEMENTS

A. STATEWIDE LIBRARY COOPERATION

The South Carolina State Library has a proactive role in developing initiatives and strategies to assure that libraries statewide, regardless of type, interact to obtain the maximum benefit from their collections and offer services to meet the needs of the citizens of South Carolina.

Goal 2. Promote library services and reading throughout the state as an integral component of the educational process and as a contributor to the economic development of the state.

Objectives:

a.   Develop a three-year plan for the Library of Congress designated Center for the Book.

b.   Develop an operational plan for the State Library Foundation.

Goal 3.   Develop strategies for increasing funding for libraries in South   Carolina.

Objectives:

a.   Decrease the State Library's dependency upon federal funds for operations.

STRATEGIC GOAL D: ENCOURAGE COOPERATION AMONG LIBRARIES OF ALL TYPES

Goal 1.   Encourage the development of library networks for resource sharing.

Objectives:

a.   Conduct a study of interlibrary loan activity in South Carolina public libraries.

b.   Investigate the feasibility of the use of shared information databases on a statewide basis.

Goal 2. Cooperate with other agencies within the State's information and telecommunications infrastructure to ensure that libraries are included in all statewide initiatives.

Objectives:

a.   Assure that State Library staff serve on state government teams/committees involved with information management and delivery.

STRATEGIC GOAL E: CONTINUOUSLY IMPROVE STATE LIBRARY OPERATIONS AND SERVICES

Goal 1.   Operate as a total quality management agency.

Objectives:

a.   Prepare a staff development policy and implementation procedures.

Goal 2. Provide policies, plans, physical facilities, and equipment for State Library operations.

Objectives:

a.   Conduct a feasibility study on facilities for Senate Street building and DBPH.

Approved by the State Library Board July 24, 1996.

Chapter III: The Network Mission and Guiding Principles

The development of a sound, carefully-crafted and forward-looking infrastructure for Indiana's Library and Information Network is the focus of this report. This plan envisions the formation of an integrated statewide network which will lay the foundation for the delivery of new and innovative resource sharing programs, services and projects to Indiana residents. For this reason, we recommend that this plan be incorporated as part of the Indiana State Library's Long-Range Plan. As a major new component of Indiana's comprehensive state plan, we assume it will be accompanied by other components as these are developed under the guidance of the Indiana State Library.

Throughout our planning process, a major effort has been to respond to the challenge of improving the coordination and delivery of network services through the integration of Indiana's ten Library Services Authorities (LSAs). After more than a year of intensive study, this report identifies reorganization of Indiana's LSAs into a single network authority as the initial planning task. Once this consolidation is realized, the New Network will be in a position to effect the accompanying transition service plan and set the stage for a new era of Indiana library networking by helping each member institution realize its potential for service in a rapidly changing world.

We believe this plan demonstrates that the Interim Group has successfully dealt with three major challenges over the course of this process, which has sought to enhance coordination of statewide network services. These challenges were:

> To broaden the vision of resource sharing.
>
> To incorporate new concepts of end user access.
>
> To reorganize network components to maximize the use of state funds.

The Network Mission:

A key starting point of the planning process was the crafting of a new mission statement that would refocus the network and its member institutions on their basic reason for existence: The improvement of services to library and information users. The New Network Mission Statement is:

> **The Network assures that all Indiana residents receive the best possible library and information services by providing a cooperative, statewide structure for information and resource sharing.**

Network Service Goals: An Overview

Goal 1: Information Access

Through the Network, end users will have the benefit of integrated statewide resource sharing systems by which to identify, access, and retrieve needed information resources.

To achieve this goal by the end of 1996, the Network will:

1.1: Support public access to the Internet and provide guidance in the use of the electronic superhighway.

1.2: Strengthen the interlibrary loan capabilities of member libraries in order that end users can secure needed information and resources not available at their local library.

1.3: Coordinate timely, cost-effective delivery of information and materials through physical and electronic means.

1.4: Provide member libraries assistance in meeting the general and specialized information retrieval and reference needs of end users.

1.5: Achieve a statewide library borrowing program that allows all users to have access to materials and information regardless of where they live or where the material is located.

1.6: Expand distance learning opportunities available to end users.

1.7: Promote end user education to assure efficient use of Network services and access to the collective resources of the membership.

Goal 2: Resource Development

The Network will enhance the ability of member libraries to contribute to, and participate in, local, state and national resource sharing initiatives.

To achieve this goal by the end of 1996, the Network will:

2.1: Provide ways by which member libraries can identify and gain access to resources held by Indiana libraries through their contributions to, and participation in, state database development.

2.2: Act as a stimulus for the development of community "freenets."

2.3: Educate and train librarians and support staff to act as intermediaries in connecting end users to local, state and global information resources— and to use appropriate information technologies.

2.4: Promote the availability of distance learning opportunities for library personnel statewide.

2.5: Provide consultation and mentoring services to facilitate member library participation in resource sharing, the adoption of new technologies, and the use of network programs and services.

2.6: Develop, manage and evaluate appropriate cooperative contracting and procurement opportunities for the membership in order to save money, promote cooperative projects, and use resources more effectively.

Goal 3: Network Development

The Network will conduct research and participate in planning to improve information access and to further information resource development.

To achieve this goal by the end of 1996, the Network will:

3.1: Sponsor market research and participate in planning in order to target priority network services for end users and member libraries.

3.2: Plan for network development and assist with statewide planning through collaboration with end users and representatives from member libraries and other agencies.

3.3: Promote the use of new technologies which demonstrate promise for improving state resource sharing programs.

3.4: Promote the development of state, national, and international standards and guidelines and work to promote their use within the Network.

3.5: Participate in the development of state and national information policy.

3.6: Act as an advocate for libraries and end users at the local, state and national levels.

3.7: Cultivate information partnerships with libraries and civic, business, education and government groups.

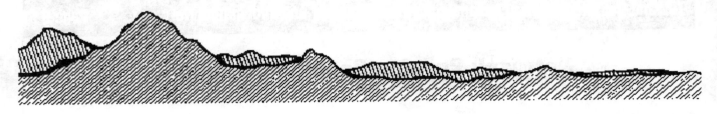

Welcome To The
SouthWest Regional Library Service System Pages.

Enhanced for Netscape® v. 1.2 or better.
HTML from The Teahouse of Experience® by Dr. John Griffiths: (grifftoe@csn.net)

1995-96
DIRECTORY OF MEMBERS AND SERVICES

Including manuals, codes, statewide agency information and a handy, clickable, Member Library Listing by Name

> The information in these pages has been supplied by SWRLSS members.
> While every effort has been made to ensure accuracy mistakes are inevitable.
> So, please check your agency's listings and bring any errors to our attention.
> **Thank you.**
> *Send corrections, comments and suggestions to sjulrich@frontier.net*

INDEX

SWRLSS Documents: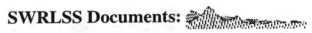

- About The SWRLSS Pages
- SWRLSS:
- **SWRLSS,** Office Staff and Addresses
- SWRLSS Services and Governing Board
- SWRLSS Long Range and Action/Work Plans for FY 1995-96
  - *Note: The SWRLSS plans are presented in a Table -*
    if your browser doesn't support Tables please request a text copy from SWRLSS
- SWRLSS Bylaws

Directories:

- Member Library Listing by Name
- Membership Listing by City
- FAX Numbers

05/19/97 17:34:58

- ○ <u>Courier Codes</u>
- ○ Internet <u>E-mail Addresses</u>
- ○ Membership <u>Listing by Type</u>
- ○ <u>MARMOT and 4-letter Codes</u> for SWRLSS Members

Manuals:

- ○ <u>Interlibrary Loan Manual</u>
- ○ <u>Cataloging Manual</u>

Statewide Information:

- ● Colorado Library <u>Organizations and Agencies</u>
- ● Colorado Cooperative <u>Purchasing Agreements</u>

Glossary of <u>Common Library and Computer Terms</u>

About The SWRLSS Pages

We have turned our printed directory into a set of world-wide-web pages! We will continue to distribute the printed directory every winter but we can make changes to the information in these pages quite easily, so, help us stay up to date - please send us any changes or corrections. You can e-mail us at: <u>sjulrich@frontier.net</u>, thanks!

You can find information by choosing links from the **INDEX.**
There are links to the Index and to the Directories throughout these pages:

The Directories list members by Name, by City, and by Type. There are also directories of FAX Numbers, Courier Codes , Internet E-mail Addresses and MARMOT and 4-letter Codes.

You will also find the Inter Library Loan and Cataloging manuals, statewide agency listings, purchasing agreements, and a Glossary in these pages.

Branch information for Public Libraries is listed in the main library entry. School libraries are listed with their Districts. The administration portion of each entry lists school Superintendents, Board Presidents, & Administrators. Membership Council representatives are appointed by each agency's governing body and are official spokes-persons for that library in System matters. Only current representatives are listed.

1. Individuals' internet e-mail addresses are in this format: (<u>sjulrich@frontier.net</u>) **and, if your browser supports e-mail, are clickable.**
2. **** THIS SHOULD ALSO REFLECT THE HYPERSTRUCTURE ****
   Automation activity for member libraries can be found in the index instead of in a separate section.

Look under index terms "*software --,*" "*online services,*" "*CD-ROM titles,*" and "*Circulation/Public Access Catalogs.*"

HERE IS A SAMPLE OF THE COMMON INFORMATION AND FORMAT FOR LIBRARY ENTRIES:
*Note: you might get better justification if you maximize your browser's window and set your browser's **fixed font** to Courier 8 point.*

TOWN

```
LIBRARY NAME                              LIBRARY TYPE
Street Address              CLC (for Colorado Library Card participants)
                                  (for schools this is the Administration bui:
                                     Courier code:  Syst.Code - Lib.Code

Mailing Address/P.O. Box
City, State Zip
                                 Council Representative/Term of Office
ADMINISTRATION
     Chair/Superintendent, Title      NAME
LIBRARY STAFF
     Director/Librarian, Title        NAME (Internet E-Mail address -- where applicabl

     Assistants/Librarians, Title     NAME . . . . . . . . . . . Modem Number

HOURS:
AUTOMATION AND NETWORKING:  Listing of computer equipment, software, and
what it is used for.
```

 Member's World-Wide-Web sites are linked.

⬛ Membership Listing by City

ALAMOSA
ADAMS STATE COLLEGE LIBRARY
ALAMOSA SCHOOL DISTRICT Re-11J
SAN LUIS VALLEY BOCES
SOUTHERN PEAKS PUBLIC LIBRARY
ANTONITO
SOUTH CONEJOS SCHOOL DISTRICT Re-10
BAYFIELD
PINE RIVER PUBLIC LIBRARY DISTRICT/BAYFIELD PUBLIC LIBRARY
BAYFIELD SCHOOL DISTRICT 10JT-R
BLANCA
SIERRA GRANDE SCHOOL DISTRICT R-30
CENTER
CENTER CONSOLIDATED SCHOOL DISTRICT 26JT
CENTER BRANCH, SAGUACHE COUNTY PUBLIC LIBRARY
CORTEZ
CROW CANYON ARCHAEOLOGICAL RESEARCH LIBRARY
CORTEZ PUBLIC LIBRARY
MONTEZUMA-CORTEZ SCHOOL DISTRICT Re-1

The SWRLSS Pages

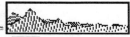

Member List <u>by City</u> ● . . . Member List <u>by Type</u> ● . . . <u>FAX Numbers</u> 📄
Library <u>List by Name</u> ● . . . Member <u>Codes</u> 🔑
Members' <u>Email Addresses</u> �';. . . . . . To the <u>Index</u> ◆

SWRSS Long Range Plan and Action/Work Plans for 1995-96

*Note: The SWRLSS plans are presented in a **Table** -
if your browser doesn't support **Tables** please request a text copy from <u>SWRLSS</u>*

MISSION STATEMENT:

SWRLSS will strengthen, support, and equalize member library services by providing leadership and encouraging cooperation among libraries in order to improve public access to information.

GOALS	STRATEGIES	ACTION/WORK PLANS
LEADERSHIP: Define, communicate, and promote the role of systems, libraries and librarians	Keep abreast of evolving trends in library and media centers	Ongoing activity: Staff read literature, attend conferences and workshops, keep people networks active.
		Special focus: SWRLSS staff continue to learn as much about automation and• technology as possible.
	Advocate directions for library development	Actively work on Colorado's new long range plan effort
		Work to integrate SWRLSS programs into state's long range plan Strategy: Contract with consulting firm to conduct needs analysis of member libraries [focus groups envisioned], leading to revision of system plan. "What do you need in order to comply with Strategies 2001?"is the approach envisioned.
		Assist in implementation of standards-based education
GOALS	STRATEGIES	ACTION/WORK PLANS
LEADERSHIP *(continued)*	Actively participate in regional and statewide committees and organizations	Known at this time: Ulrich: CCLD [including chairing Long Range Planning Committee], "Fourteeners" meetings, System Directors, MARMOT council
		Griffiths: GorILLa committe, SCAN Steering committee

05/19/97 17:35:41

	Connect member libraries with each other, SWRLSS, and outside entities.	Maintain fax, internet, newsletter, 800#, courier, and BBS activity.
		Expand internet communication, implementing SWRLSS home page on WWW.
		Screen and forward timely information from variety of communications, including listservs and mailings to members, usually via email or fax
		Encourage internet participation by providing trial period of internet accounts to libraries not yet using them
		Provide internet accounts for governing board members
GOALS	**STRATEGIES**	**ACTION/WORK PLANS**
LEADERSHIP *(continued)*	Continue publications	Continue newsletter
		Enhance publications and office efficiency by purchasing new scanner
		Turn the SWRLSS Directory into a more of a handbook and provide more outreach to members by having board members take the new handbook to member libraries.
	Continue promotional activities	Conduct semi-annual bookmark design contest to promote both member libraries as well as SWRLSS itself
	Publicize successes	Newsletter; contact with legislators; contact with citizens and librarians; annual report to the State Library.
	Provide access to regional/statewide cooperative projects and grants	Offer grants to member libraries for cooperative projects between two or more agencies, thus helping them fulfill portions of Strategies 2001
GOALS	**STRATEGIES**	**ACTION/WORK PLANS**
SERVICES -- Enhance and improve the services offered by member libraries..	Offer training and assistance for varying constituencies within member libraries.	Actually hold SWRLSS School Reprise, for rural public library directors [held over from previous fiscal year]
		Enhance members' problem-solving skills by giving consultation and advice.
		Provide mini-grants for member libraries to attend continuing education events out system area

Long Range Plan
1996-2001

Contents

Purpose

The Central Minnesota Libraries Exchange, commonly known as CMLE, is a voluntary association of independent library/media, information entities, joined together under the provisions of Minnesota Statutes 134.351, subd. 1 for the benefits of cooperation to include but not be limited to resource sharing, long-range planning, delivery systems, bibliographic databases, and communication systems.

Back to Contents

Introduction

This long-range plan is understood to be a guide for implementing programs currently found to be

05/19/97 17:43:31

SEFLINK

Southeast Florida Library Information Network

SEFLIN Member Libraries ONLY

About SEFLIN

People & Institutions

- Board of Directors
- SEFLIN Member Institutions
- SEFLIN Committees
- SEFLIN Staff Directory

Member Library Services & Publications

- Calendar of Events
- Summary of Services
- Committee Directories and Publications
- Listservs
- Member Newsletter
- SEFLIN Long Range Strategic Plan 1996-2000 (full)
- SEFLIN Long Range Strategic Plan 1996-2000 (abbreviated)

Positions Available at SEFLIN

- Information Instruction & Training Specialist
- Associate Director of Public Services
- Network Technologist for Free-Net

SEFLIN Free-Net Home Page | Top of This Section | HELP
Index & Internet Search Tools |

SEFLIN Menu = ([   ]) [Now]

The SEFLIN Free-Net is sponsored, operated, and governed by the Southeast
Florida Library Information Network [SEFLIN], a non-profit organization
of libraries in Broward, Dade, Palm Beach, Martin & Monroe counties.

05/19/97 17:39:44

Plan 2000

The AMIGOS Strategic Plan for 1995~2000

> **Our Strategic Vision**
> **Guiding Principles**
> **Our Mission**
> **Goals and Objectives**
> **The Tradition of AMIGOS**

Our Strategic Vision

The AMIGOS Board of Trustees entered the final decade of the century with a commitment to change in ways that strengthen the Network and thus enhance each member's ability to benefit from belonging to AMIGOS. Our strategic vision is a Service Vision: AMIGOS serves those who serve others. At AMIGOS, we respect and serve libraries, seeking to assist them in meeting their goals effectively, creatively, and affordably. We respect the value that libraries bring to their various communities, and work collaboratively to support libraries and enhance their ability to serve society.

Expanding our service offerings. . .modernizing our technical support bases. . .extending our organizational partnerships. . .all these enhance our ability to assist member libraries in applying information technologies to serve their users.

During 1995-2000, AMIGOS will continue to explore technology-based distance learning options for members. We will assist members to employ additional information technologies, with a special focus on imaging applications for libraries. We will seek even greater economies in purchasing power for our recently expanded member base. As citizens of the Southwest move ever more quickly into the Information Age and tap into international electronic networks for information delivery, Southwestern libraries must provide guidance, access, and service. AMIGOS will assist member libraries to provide that service.

AMIGOS' continuing role is to facilitate cooperation among members, provide information and support, negotiate favorable prices from information service providers, and expand members' service capabilities through staff training. Ours is an exciting, challenging, and rewarding service role.

Bonnie Juergens
AMIGOS Executive Director ✦

Guiding Principles

Provide cost-effective technology-based services responsive to the needs of libraries and other consumers of information, and exercise regular review and update of service lines to ensure that locally developed or brokered products continue to meet the needs of members.

Promote, develop, and support programs devoted to preservation and cooperative use of member resources.

Provide cost-effective, innovative training and support programs to strengthen libraries' implementation of information technologies.

Maintain member loyalty and support by meeting member needs in a cooperative, open, and participative manner.

Maintain a balanced operating budget with adequate working capital, human resources, and facilities. ✦

Our Mission

The mission of AMIGOS is to:

- Provide innovative information services,
- Promote regional cooperation and resource-sharing, and
- Support libraries as leaders in education and information services. ✦

Goals and Objectives

Facilitate the ability of libraries to provide timely, convenient, cost-effective access to information regardless of format, content, or location.

- Provide high quality information services that meet industry standards and convey a price advantage due to economies of scale available through AMIGOS membership.
- Provide libraries access to experts to support efficient, cost-effective integration and implementation of information systems.
- Inform members of information technology research initiatives to assist their technology decision-making.
- Assist libraries to develop programs that facilitate patron abilities to utilize emerging information technologies.

Assist libraries to play a leadership role in the information industry and in the development of national information policy.

- Promote awareness, among librarians and the broader information community, of the need for libraries to be active participants in national, regional, and state initiatives and policy decisions concerning information and telecommunications technology.
- Inform members of information industry standards development and provide services responsive to standards.
- Promote member awareness of information industry activities.

Aggressively develop, independently and in partnership with libraries and other information providers, new services for libraries and other consumers of information.

- Monitor information and telecommunication industries and pursue appropriate service development partnerships.
- Refine internal processes for identifying, assessing, and providing new services.
- Develop new services which enhance the information dissemination role of libraries.
- Focus on development and provision of services that help libraries go beyond bibliography to electronic provision of full text and imaging.
- Strengthen AMIGOS' role as a value-adding broker by working closely with OCLC and other partners in the development of end-user services.

Provide services to non-library entities and individuals in ways that support and enhance member library services.

- Explore development of a non-voting member category for non-library entities and individuals.
- Expand awareness of AMIGOS and its member libraries in non-library industries and among individual consumers.
- Explore expansion of services to the records management industry. ✦

The Tradition of AMIGOS

AMIGOS Bibliographic Council, Inc. was formed in 1974 when 22 libraries joined together to bring OCLC access to the Southwest. The group chose the name AMIGOS which means friends in Spanish to reflect a cooperative spirit and dedication to resource sharing. Today, AMIGOS continues the technology-based resource-sharing tradition of its founders.

The AMIGOS Membership comprises over 500 libraries located primarily in the southwestern United States. As a nonprofit organization, AMIGOS has grown to be a leader in library information technology and one of the nation s largest library service networks. AMIGOS serves its member libraries by providing:

OCLC Access
Training Sessions and Workshops
Technical Support Publications
AMIGOS Consulting Service
AMIGOS A-Plus Services
Automation Services
Member Discounts
Reference Databases

05/19/97 17:44:59

REFERENCES

1. AMIGOS, *Plan 2000 The AMIGOS Strategic Plan for 1995-2000*, 1995.
   Park Central Dr., Suite 500, Dallas, TX 75251

2. Bergen County Cooperative Library System (BCCLS), *Mission Statement/Plan of Service*, 1996.
   Main St., Hackensack, NJ 07601-4802

3. Bibliographical Center For Research, Rocky Mountain Region, Inc. (BCR), *BCR's Mission Statement*, 1996.
   14394 East Evans Ave., Aurora, CO 80014-1478

4. Black Gold Cooperative Library System, *Mission Statement*, 1996.
   4882 McGrath Street, Suite 230, Ventura, CA 93003

5. Boston Library Consortium (BLC), *Strategic Plan Summary*, 1996.
   666 Boylston St., Rm. 317, Boston, MA 02117

6. California State Library, *Strategic Plan*, 1995-2000.
   P O Box 942837, Sacramento, CA 94237-0001

7. Center For Research Libraries, *Meeting the Challenge Strategic Plan 1997-2001*, 1996.
   6050 South Kenwood, Chicago, IL 60637-2804

8. Central Colorado Library System (CCLS), *FY 1997 Annual Plan and Budget Request/Incorporating the Long Range Plan for FY 1998 and FY 1999*, 1996.
   4350 Wadsworth, No. 340, Wheat Ridge, CO 80033-4638

9. Central Florida Library Cooperative (CFLC), *Strategic Plan*, 1995.
   431 East Horatio Ave., Suite 230, Maitland, FL 32751

10. Central Jersey Regional Library Cooperative - Region V,
    a. *Strategic Plan for Automation & Technology for the Central Jersey Regional Library Cooperative 1995-1997*, 1995.
    b. *Long Range Strategic Plan 1993-1998*, 1993.
    4400 Route 9 South, Freehold, NJ 07728-2942

11. Central Minnesota Libraries Exchange (CMLE), *CMLE Long Range Plan 1996-2001*, 1996.
    Centennial Hall, Rm. 61, Saint Cloud State University, Saint Cloud, MN 56301-4498

12. Cleveland Area Metropolitan Library System (CAMLS), *CAMLS Strategic Plan*, 1994-1997.
    20600 Chagrin Blvd, Suite 500, Shaker Heights, OH 44122-5334

13. Colorado Alliance Of Research Libraries (CARL), *CARL Strategic Plan*, 1996.
    3801 East Florida Ave., Suite 515, Denver, CO 80210

14. Connecticut State Library, *A Five-Year Strategic Plan*, 1990-1995.
    231 Capitol Ave., Hartford, CT 06106-1537

15. Council Of Wisconsin Libraries, Inc. (COWL), *Strategic Plan for Information Access & Resource Sharing: Year 2000*, 1995.
    728 State St., Rm. 464, Madison, WI 53706-1494

16. Delaware Division Of Libraries, State Library, *Annual Report*, 1996.
    Dept. of State, 43 South DuPont Hwy, Dover, DE 19901

17. Florida Network Planning Task Force and the State Library of Florida, *Florida Plan for Interlibrary Cooperation, Resource Sharing & Network Development*, 1994.
    R.A. Gray Building, Tallahassee, FL 32301

18. Georgia Department of Education, Public Library Services, *Long-Range Program for Georgia Public Libraries*, 1995-1999.
    156 Trinity Avenue, SW, Atlanta, GA 30303-3692

19. Greater Cincinnati Library Consortium, *Long-Range Plan FY 1997/98 - FY 1999/2000*, 1996.
    3333 Vine St, Suite 605, Cincinnati, OH 45220-2214

20. High Plains Regional Library Service System, *Long Range Plan*, 1997-1999.
    800 Eighth Ave., Suite 341, Greeley, CO 80631

21. Indiana State Library, *Toward the Integration of Indiana's Statewide Library and Information Network: A Final Report and Plan*, 1994.
    140 North Senate Ave., Indianapolis, IN 46204

22. Indianapolis Foundation Library Fund Eligible Libraries, *Strategic Plan 1995-2010*, 1995
    Indianapolis, IN 46204

23. Kentucky Department For Libraries & Archives, *KDLA*, 1996.
    300 Coffee Tree Road, PO Box 537, Frankfort, KY 40602-0537

24. Lakeland Library Cooperative, *Final Report, Long-Range Plan*, 1994.
    5 Lyon St., Suite 320, Grand Rapids, MI 49503

25. Library Of Michigan,
    a. *LSCA Long Range Program*, 1996-1999.
    b. *Shaping the Future: Michigan's Emerging Information Infrastructure*, 1996.
    c. *Request for Proposals*, 1997.
       717 W Allegan Ave., PO Box 30007, Lansing, MI 48909

26. Massachusetts Board of Library Commissioners, *A Strategic Plan For The Future of Library Services In Massachusets*, 1993.
    648 Beacon Street, Boston, MA 02215

27. Michigan Library Association, *Initial Report Action Plan for Michigan Libraries*, 1994.
    1000 Long Boulevard, Suite 1, Lansing, MI 48911

28. Meridian Library System, *1995-1997 System Strategic Plan*, 1995.
    3423 Second Avenue, Suite 301, Kearney, NE 68847

29. METRONET,
    a. *Federal Grant Application FY 1997*, 1997.
    b. *State Grant Application FY 1997*, 1997.
       Suite 116, 2324 University Ave., West, St. Paul, MN 55114

30. Minuteman Library Network, *Strategic Plan*, 1994-1998.
    4 California Ave., 5th floor., Framingham, MA 01701-8867

31. MOLO Regional Library System, *MOLO's Strategic Roles Plan: 1996-99*, 1996.
    Monroe Mall, 1260 Monroe Ave., New Philadelphia, OH 44663-4147

32. Nebraska Library Commission, *Nebraska Long Range Plan for Library and Information Services*, 1997-1999.
    The Atrium, 1200 North Street, Suite 120, Lincoln, NE 68508-2023

33. Network Of Alabama Academic Libraries (NAAL), *Annual Plan*, 1996-1997.
    c/o Alabama Commission on Higher Education, PO Box 302000, Montgomery, AL 36130- 2000

34. Nevada State Library and Archives,
    a. *Nevada Libraries Continuing Education Plan*, 1995.
    b. *Long-Range Plan*, 1991-1995.
    c. *Master Plan*, 1993-1996.
    d. *CLAN Automation Plan*, 1992.
       Capitol Complex, Carson City, NV 89710

35. New Hampshire State Library, *Gateway 2000 A Strategic Plan for the New Hampshire Automated Information System*, 1993.
    20 Park Street, Concord, NH 03301-6314

36. New Jersey State Library, *Libraries 2000: New Jersey's Technology Plan for Libraries in the 21st Century*, 1996.
    Department of Education, 185 West State Street, CN 520, Trenton, NJ 08625-0520

37. North Country Library Cooperative, *Long Range Plan*, 1997-2002.
    820 North Ninth Street, Virginia, MN 55792

38. North Country Reference & Research Resources Council, *Strategic Plan of Development*, 1996-2000.
    7 Commerce Lane, Canton, NY 13617

39. North Dakota State Library, *Library Vision 2004*, 1996.
    604 East Boulevard Ave., Bismarck, ND 58505-0800

40. North East Wisconsin Intertype Libraries, Inc., Nicolet Federated Library System, *NEWIL Area Plan*, 1996.
    515 Pine St., Green Bay, WI 54301-5194

41. Northeast Kansas Library System, *Long Range Plan 1996-1998*, 1996.
    3301 Clinton Parkway Court, Suite 6, Lawrence, KS 66047

42. Oregon State Library, *Goals and Objectives for the State Library in 1995-1997*, 1995.
    State Library Bldg., 250 Winter Street, N.E., Salem, OR 97310-0640

43. PALINET, *Linking to the Twenty-First Century*, 1995.
    3401 Market St., Suite 262, Philadelphia, PA 19104

44. Pennsylvania Community College Library Consortium, *Establishing A Vision*, 1993.
    Bucks County Community College, Swamp Road, Newtown, PA 18940

45. River Bend Library System, *RBLS Service Manual: A User's Guide to System Services*, 1995.
    P.O. Box 125, 220 West 23rd Avenue, Coal Valley, IL 61240

46. Rochester Regional Library Council (RRLC), *Informing Our Future: The Rochester Regional Library Council 2000 Report*, 1994.
    390 Packetts Landing, PO Box 66160, Fairport, NY 14450

47. South Carolina State Library, *Strategic Plan*, 1996-1999.
    1500 Senate St., PO Box 11469, Columbia, SC 29211-1469

48. South Central Research Library Council, *Seven Strategic Directions*, 1993.
   215 North Cayuga St., Ithaca, NY 14850

49. South Dakota State Library, *SDLN Strategic Plan*, 1995.
   Mercedes MacKay Bldg., 800 Governors Drive, Pierre, SD 57501-2294

50. Southeast Florida Library Information Network, Inc. (SEFLIN),
   a. *New Horizons for SEFLIN, 2000, LRSP 1996-2000*, 1996.
   b. *LRSP Summary*
      100 S Andrews Ave., Fort Lauderdale, FL 33301

51. Southeast Nebraska Library System, *Plan for Service 1995-1997*, 1995-1997.
   Union College Library, 3800 South 48th St., Lincoln, NE 68506

52. Southeastern Library Network, Inc., (SOLINET), *SOLINET: Mapping the future*, 1995
      1438 West Peachtree St., NW, Suite 200, Atlanta, GA 30309-2955

53. Southwest Area Multi-County Multi-Type Interlibrary Exchange (SAMMIE), *Long Range Plan 1996-2001*, 1996.
   Southwest State University Library, Marshall, MN 56258

54. Southwest Regional Library Service System (SWRLSS), *Long Range Plan FY 1997-1999*, 1996.
   P O Drawer B, Durango, CO 81302

55. Tampa Bay Library Consortium, Inc. (TBLC),
   a. *Linking Libraries and People Strategic Plan*, 1995-2000.
   b. SUNLINE Libraries, *Strategic Directions for the SUNLINE Libraries*, 1995.
      10002 Princess Palm Ave., Suite 124, Tampa, FL 33619

56. Tennessee State Library and Archives,
   a. *Long Range Program for Library Services and Development*, 1996-2001.
   b. *Multi-County Regional Library Long-Range Planning Goals and Objectives*, 1996-97.
      403 Seventh Avenue North, Nashville, TN 37243-0312

57. Washington Research Library Consortium (WRLC), *Strategic Plan*, 1996.
   901 Commerce Dr., Upper Marlboro, MD 20772

58. Worcester Area Cooperating Libraries, *Multi-Year Plan*, 1995-97.
   486 Changler Street, Worcester, MA 01602